WILDLIFE WARRIOR

Richard Shears

WILDLIFE WARRIOR

Steve Irwin: 1962–2006
A Man Who Changed the World

NEW
HOLLAND

First published in Australia in 2006 by
New Holland Publishers (Australia) Pty Ltd
Sydney • Auckland • London • Cape Town

www.newholland.com.au

14 Aquatic Drive Frenchs Forest NSW 2086 Australia
218 Lake Road Northcote Auckland New Zealand
86 Edgware Road London W2 2EA United Kingdom
80 McKenzie Street Cape Town 8001 South Africa

National Library of Australia Cataloguing-in-Publication Data:

Shears, Richard, 1944–
Wildlife Warrior : Steve Irwin 1962–2006 A man who changed the world.

ISBN 9781741105520.

1. Irwin, Steve, 1962-2006. 2. Herpetologists - Australia -
Biography. 3. Conservationists - Australia - Biography.
4. Naturalists - Australia - Biography. 5. Zoologists -
Australia - Biography. 6. Television personalities -
Australia - Biography. I. Title.

597.9092

Publisher: Martin Ford
Production controller: Linda Bottari
Project Editor: Michael McGrath
Designer: Greg Lamont
Cover image: APL, from *The Crocodile Hunter: Collision Course*.
Picture Research: Richard Shears, Michael McGrath
Printer: Griffin Press, Adelaide, South Australia

This book is dedicated to Steve Irwin's dream:

a world where wild animals

are no longer threatened with extinction.

Acknowledgements

Special thanks are due to my wife, Isobelle, who worked tirelessly with me on this book. Through her own devoted work in caring for the broken, lost and abandoned creatures of our urban environment she led me to understand how no animal in distress can be ignored. There isn't a vet for miles around who doesn't know her.

Apart from information gained from my own meeting with Steve and numerous visits to his zoo over the years, I have drawn details for this book from a large number of sources. For it seemed that no matter what corner of the world I looked, there was always something to be gleaned about Steve. He was everywhere, bursting with enthusiasm about his work to save our wildlife.

Acknowledgements for help and for background material are also due to the following, with apologies if anyone has been overlooked: Cameron Laird, photographer, Townsville; News Ltd. Newspapers—*Courier Mail*, *Sunday Mail*, *Daily Telegraph*, Sydney; *The Scientific American*; The Discovery Channel; *Animal Planet*; *New York Times*; *Washington Post*; The BBC; CNN; *Sydney Morning Herald*; Andrew Denton, through his talk show *Enough Rope*; *marie claire*; *Who*; *New Idea*; *Woman's Day*; Peter Carrette of Icon Images, Sydney; Channel Nine, Sydney; Channel Seven, Sydney; Channel Ten, Sydney; Steve and Terri Irwin's own book, *The Crocodile Hunter*, published by Viking 1997 & 2001.

Thanks also to Tim Curnow and the dedicated team at New Holland.

Contents

1

And the World Stopped

I had a head-on car collision in 1996. I was driving along doing the normal speed and this car had a blow-out and lost control. It hit me head-on and I was knocked out. When I came to, I saw my dog Sui was knocked out. I pulled her out and the cars caught on fire. That's why I'm not that worried about getting killed by animals.

There are moments in history that touch even the most ordinary of people. They do not need to have been there. They did not have to be a witness to the assassination of President Kennedy to feel the effect of his death on their lives, even if for a passing moment the news froze them as they went about their daily tasks. They did not have to be a fan to recall where they were when Elvis Presley died. They did not need to have personally known Princess Diana to have felt the shock as radio and television news broadcasts announced that she had died in a car crash. The outpouring of grief over her death swept around the world and even the hardest of men found themselves weeping.

Then, of course, there were the attacks on America. We will all remember what we were doing when we heard that the twin towers had been brought down by aircraft hijacked by terrorists, resulting in the deaths of nearly 3000 people. The story dominated the news bulletins for months. Thirteen months later, there was the Bali bombings when terrorists killed more than 200 people at two popular nightspots. Many of us can remember, too, what we were doing when we heard the news. And where we were when we learned of the terrorist attacks in London in 2005.

Such global shock and sadness comes only rarely. Kennedy, Elvis and Diana have gone, the mourning is long over in many cases and while it continued for families and friends who will never forget their loved ones, the world's focus turned on terrorism in faraway trouble spots in the Middle East, Afghanistan and Iraq.

On Monday, 4 September, 2006, it was 'business as usual' around the world. A British tourist was shot dead and a Dutch tourist, two British women, a New Zealand woman and a policeman were wounded when a lone gunman opened fire on them at a Roman amphitheatre in the Jordanian capital, Amman. Rock star Pete Doherty, frontman of The Babyshambles and boyfriend of model Kate Moss, managed to avoid jail in London after a judge told him she was impressed with his attempts to come off drugs. South of London, police were continuing to investigate an Islamic school in Sussex believed to have been used as an al-Qaeda training camp.

Across the Atlantic, six siblings—children of a Mexican immigrant—died in a house fire believed to have been caused by a candle. In China it was reported that 23 people had been killed in three separate mining accidents in recent days, while from Bucharest it was reported that vulnerable Romanian children abandoned in institutions were being offered for sale for a few thousand US dollars. In Spain, police rounded up more than 1100 Africans attempting to reach the Canary Islands after long and dangerous trips in over-crowded boats that had set out from Mauritania. From Dakar came a report that eight crew members of a trawler had been thrown into the sea to drown after being attacked by fishermen from another boat. In sport, André Agassi said goodbye to tennis, the sport he had dominated for so many years, when he was knocked out of the US Open.

Australia's focus was on their own tennis star, Lleyton Hewitt, who was nursing a dodgy knee as he prepared to step onto the Flushing Meadows court, while on the domestic front sub-editors began working on the story of the death of 85-year-old Colin Thiele, author of the Australian children's classic *Storm Boy*.

These were the stories that were scoured by news desks across the globe and it was a question of picking the best of them and deciding where they would be placed in the news pages or how high up they would be on the list of items to be read by news broadcasters.

Suddenly the routine changed direction—dramatically.

A shocking story began to emerge. At first radio announcers dared not breathe a name in case the reports were wrong. Something terrible had happened in Australia's tropical north. It was early in the afternoon and the story began to pick up pace and magnitude.

And then the world stopped.

Steve Irwin, the famous Crocodile Hunter and irrepressible wildlife campaigner was dead. Steve Irwin, the popular conservationist who was always instantly recognisable in his khaki shirt and shorts and who made the exclamation 'Crikey!' an international catchword as he wrestled huge man-eating crocodiles and poisonous snakes, had been killed in the most bizarre manner.

Initially, reaction to his death was united in the same assumption—he must have been killed by a crocodile. Then came the incredible confirmation: he had been stabbed through the heart by a stingray. In their wildest dreams no-one could have imagined him meeting his fate underwater and certainly not in a deadly strike by a fish.

The news sped around the world on the wires, stunning everyone who saw the words flash up on their computer screens. It was, of course, the dead of night or early evening in most parts of the northern hemisphere and it was not until early morning in Europe that the news reached into homes and offices.

The phone in my hotel room in London, where I was on a brief business trip after flying there from my home in Australia, jolted me from my sleep early on the morning of Monday, 4 September. It was then afternoon of the same day in Australia.

'Quick, quick!' urged my wife Isobelle, calling from Sydney. 'Switch on the news!'

I grabbed the remote control and switched on the BBC world news … and caught the tail end of a story that took a moment to absorb. 'Mr Irwin was struck in the chest and is believed to have died instantly …' Then there was file footage of Steve Irwin. Steve Irwin the Crocodile Hunter wrestling crocodiles.

'What the hell happened?' I asked my wife, who was still on the phone. 'How was he struck in the chest? Is he really dead? I don't get this. It's unbelievable.'

'It was a stingray,' said Isobelle. 'It struck him in the heart.'

We hung up and I stumbled over to my computer to call up every news service I could find, particularly the Australian newspaper websites. Why were my hands trembling? Was it because this was an incredible news story that I knew I would soon be working on with intensity for my paper, the *Daily Mail*, for the rest of the day—or was it because I had personally known Steve? I didn't know him as closely as those who have worked with him on his many adventures into the outback and in other wild regions of the world, but I'd interviewed him on several occasions and had visited his famous Australia Zoo to write stories about weird and wonderful events taking place there.

I snatched up the phone. It was still a little after 8am and no-one would be on duty yet in the news room at the *Mail*, but I knew my foreign editor, Gerry Hunt, would already be on his way in, driving down the M1 as usual.

'Gerry …' I began.

'I know,' he said. 'Steve Irwin. I've heard it on the radio. It's incredible. Bizarre. What a weird way for a lad like that to go. We're going to want a big piece from you.'

So I began pulling together a news feature for the *Daily Mail* on the Steve Irwin I knew and tried to summarise an incredible life in a relatively meagre 2000 words. How could I do justice to all that he had achieved before his life had been snuffed out at the age of 44? A man who had no less than 34 fan clubs on the Internet, not to mention the 32 dedicated to his wife Terri and their young daughter Bindi.

I was not alone in facing such a quandary. Globally, there was not a newsroom that was not pulling together every word, every picture, every video, every interview that had been written and broadcast about Steve Irwin. Adjectives, descriptions tumbled out … unabashed passion, hero, an Aussie caricature, the real deal who was at least as famous as those other Australian exports, Nicole Kidman, Kylie Minogue and Russell Crowe, if not more. He was crazy, he was fearless, invincible, a fast-talking wildlife enthusiast in khaki shirts and short shorts, whose nasal twang penetrated lounge rooms and classrooms around the world.

News of his death pushed every story, including events in Iraq, off the front pages everywhere. The shocking tragedy on the Great Barrier Reef led news bulletins on major television networks in the United States, where Iraq, Afghanistan and the Middle East usually dominate. There was only one name on everyone's lips: Steve Irwin.

From the shock and grief that swept the world, a stunning realisation was emerging. Steve Irwin was a giant. The world had lost a man of heroic proportions. The Crocodile Hunter, an uncomplicated boy from the bush, had touched and changed lives.

The *New York Times* and America's ABC made it their top story. CNN dropped other items from its website home page to make space for news of Steve, while the network's Larry King abandoned a program that had been previously scheduled to screen an interview he had with the Crocodile Hunter in 2004.

The American cable television channel Discovery, on which Steve's documentary adventures are shown, tossed aside its scheduled programs to run interviews and film of their star. In Britain *The Sun* ran a banner headline, 'Crikey, Croc Hunter Steve Killed by Stingray', which was perhaps a flippant way of announcing his death but even so the message was there.

The Daily Mail ran my story as a double-page spread under the headline: 'Deadly Last Dive of the Crocodile Man' with a subheading reading: 'Daredevil Steve Irwin killed as his heart is pierced by the barb from a giant stingray.' In that story, I told of the ebullient, unforgettable character I had known, a loveable larrikin, a real-life Crocodile Dundee who was passionate about the environment and saving the world's dying species.

Still the headlines raged. Unabated. Steve's death was the lead item on Google News, while in Berlin the newspaper *Die Welt* reported: 'He would have said: Crocs Rule.' The BBC website invited readers for their reaction and soon traffic on the reader forum was boosted by 50 per cent as fans wrote in to express their distress.

Karl Lee of Reading wrote: 'My favourite saying of his was "You're all right mate, you're all right" while holding an extremely poisonous snake which was trying to bite him. This shows the kind of guy he was.'

Steve was a household name in Britain and *The Times* newspaper reflected that in a full-page obituary which described him as 'exuberant', 'a highly knowledgeable natural historian' and 'an ambassador for conservation.'

In *The Guardian* newspaper, writer Mark Bristow reflected what many had at first thought when news of Steve's death broke—that he had been killed by one of the many dangerous creatures with which he had tempted fate. 'Reports of the Australian wildlife television presenter Steve Irwin's death have long been either exaggerated or expected,' he wrote. 'On previous occasions, Irwin, known worldwide for his Discovery Channel programs, was allegedly killed by a black mamba and a komodo dragon. This time, sadly, the reports were true—the barb from a stingray punching into his heart in what most experts regard as a freak accident.'

The respected *Washington Post*, famous for its Watergate story, told how Steve Irwin 'spent much of his life not just tempting fate but petting it, riding its back and swinging it by the tail.' Then added: 'In the end, fate snapped back. It was a freaky way to go— stingrays are rarely lethal—but perhaps morbidly fitting.'

Post's writer Paul Farhi recalled that in one episode of the show on the Animal Planet cable channel, Steve walked through a bat cave, taking a bat 'shower' in the process. 'In another segment, he combat-crawled up to a pack of vultures as they fed on the remains of a hippo.'

Then there was the *New York Times* summary, describing Steve as being famous for death-defying crocodile stunts. The paper recorded how Steve customarily appeared on American talk shows in his trademark hiking boots and khaki shorts and shirt 'commenting volubly on animal conservation and showing clips of his fearless exploits, which included leaping on the backs of crocodiles, wrestling with boas and mastering poisonous snakes and spiders.'

News of Steve Irwin's death reached the highest of places. It was talked about in Buckingham Palace and the White House. President George W Bush was among the first to send his condolences to Steve's American-born wife, Terri, saying through a White House spokesman that he was 'saddened' by the death of the Australian he had met in 2003 and he was praying for Terri and their two young children.

In homes, offices, hotels and pubs the tragedy was on everyone's lips. His name was everywhere—London, Sydney, New York, Europe, the Middle East, Africa, Asia and even in the tiny scattered islands of the Pacific Ocean. People wept. Children too, one Sydney mother recalling how her youngsters regarded Steve as part of their family and how her 11-year-old son had asked: 'Why did it have to be Steve Irwin? Why couldn't it have been someone older, like Sean Connery?'

They knew Steve Irwin not only for his death-defying feats with crocodiles and poisonous snakes but for his passion for the environ-ment and they knew him for the controversies he stirred. Will we ever forget that extraordinary scene at his Australia Zoo when he entered a crocodile enclosure with his arm wrapped around his month-old son Bob as he then proceeded to feed a dead chicken into the gaping mouth of a leaping crocodile? It was yet another story that encircled the globe and, for a time, had even his most loyal fans questioning the wisdom of the entertainment.

It was, without doubt, an error of judgement brought on, many suggested, by his determination to enlarge his profile. Yet his name and his work needed no enhancement. Everyone knew Steve Irwin as a 'true blue' Aussie, an ordinary bloke whose extraordinary actions left an indelible impression.

There would be few who would not be able to recall where they were or what they were doing when they heard that he had been killed. The international and ongoing outpouring of grief has been described as 'Diana-esque'. Almost at once fans began to stream towards his Australia Zoo in Queensland just to place flowers, cards and other simple memorials—or just to stand and breathe silent goodbyes.

So just what did happen out there on the reef to bring such a full, spirited life to such a tragic and sudden end?

2

Fatal Encounter

If something ever happens to me, people are gonna be like,
'We knew a croc would get him!'

The sleepy little resort of Port Douglas lies 60 kilometres (37 miles) north of Cairns, northern Queensland, enticing tourists from around the world as a starting point for trips out to the Great Barrier Reef. There is a friendly, village atmosphere in its main street, bustling with tourist paraphernalia and coffee shops which swell the permanent population of 4000 by many thousands during the summer season. Movie stars, disguised behind sunglasses and under baseball caps, mingle with the holiday crowds, maintaining their anonymity in luxury homes they have rented or in private quarters at the sprawling Sheraton Mirage hotel, built by the late, failed entrepreneur Christopher Skase.

Bill Clinton spent a holiday at the Sheraton and it was falsely rumoured that Monica Lewinsky had stayed there, too, on Mr Clinton's recommendation. Marlon Brando, Val Kilmer, Russell

Crowe—they've all passed through Port Douglas, taking trips out to the reef and up to the exotic Daintree Rainforest, a leisurely drive to the north.

From the marina, large motor cruisers carrying hundreds of people take tourists out to a number of coral outcrops on the reef, where they are able to dive among schools of rainbow-coloured fish. Couples from all around the world travel to the town to get married in the quaint church, St Mary's by the Sea, or on Four Mile Beach on the edge of the Coral Sea.

Yet for all its laid-back atmosphere, Port Douglas has been the centre of numerous sea dramas, one of the most memorable in recent times being the disappearance of American couple Thomas and Eileen Lonergan, aged 33 and 28, who vanished during a diving trip to St Crispin Reef, off Port Douglas, in January 1998. An inquest found later they had been left behind by their tour boat while underwater, had not been discovered missing for 48 hours and had probably been taken by sharks. Their terrible ordeal later became the inspiration for a movie, *Open Water*.

In December, 2004, a 38-year-old spear fisherman died in a pool of blood after his friends pulled him on board their boat following a shark attack at Opal Reef, 50 kilometres (31 miles) north east of Port Douglas. That incident and the presumed deaths of the Loneragans were tragic examples of the dangers that could befall anyone at any time in one of the most beautiful regions of the world.

Steve Irwin and his crew, his closest and trusted friends, arrived in Port Douglas in August on board Steve's 22-metre (72-foot) double-deck research launch, *Croc One*, which he had designed, fitting it with two floating crocodile traps, two inflatable dinghies, two shark dive cages and two cranes for lifting heavy creatures from the water.

Their plan was to film sequences around the Great Barrier Reef for an Animal Planet program. The series this time did not feature the man-eating reptiles that Steve was known to wrestle with—instead, he was looking for creatures that would match the documentary series' title, *Ocean's Deadliest*.

In the previous weeks he had been hard at work, doing what Steve Irwin was famous for—wrestling with crocodiles in the Lakefield National Park at Cape York, not just for the hell of it but because they were needed for research. The park, covering 1.3 million acres and located on the eastern side of Cape York Peninsula, is one of five regions set aside for saltwater crocodile conservation in the state of Queensland. Rangers had been monitoring their numbers and distribution over the years, but new research was always welcomed. A prime reason for keeping watch on their movements was to ensure that crocodiles and tourists did not come within close proximity. Close to 20,000 people travel to the park each year to set up their tents in one of the scores of campsites set aside in the park. They go there to fish for barramundi and take photographs of the park's incredible beauty but the burning ambition of most is to observe a crocodile in its natural habitat. While rangers are happy enough for tourists to take pictures from afar, it was important to know where crocodiles were located and in which billabong—section of a river that is cut off from the main stream—they might have built their nests, so that no human accidentally blundered into their dangerous territory.

In the five weeks he was there, accompanied by his wife Terri and their two young children, and a team including cameramen and trappers, Steve had captured no less than 32 crocodiles for tagging as part of a joint University of Queensland and Australia Zoo research project. They wanted to learn more about crocodile movements, where they swim through the swamps and creeks and how far they roam.

The crocodiles were more than 3 metres (9 feet) long and required at least three men to straddle them and hold them down while satellite tracking equipment was wired to their bodies. Young Bob and his older sister Bindi joined in, practising their own croc-catching skills—but they were doing it the safe way. Their crocodile was made of plastic. Bob would jump on the toy's back and then he'd call to his sister for help. He'd ask her to get on its back while he took the head. Then he'd bawl out to his mother to grab hold of the top jaw. Both Terri and Steve thought he was getting the hang of it.

'John,' Steve told his friend, manager and film-maker John Stainton who was on the expedition, 'I've had the best month of my life.'

'Gee, that's a big statement, Steve,' said Stainton.

'No, it's the best month of my life.'

A photograph taken on that expedition shows the contentment on Steve's face as he poses with his father, Bob and Bindi beside a mesh crocodile trap they have set up beside a river.

With those grand days and film sequences over, Steve headed south to Port Douglas, while Terri took the children home to prepare for a holiday in Tasmania.

After mooring among the many other privately-owned launches and the bigger vessels that take tourists out to the reef, Steve took a stroll along the marina, where he and his crew were to remain sleeping on board *Croc One* for five days, hoping the overcast weather would clear.

Within minutes of that first landing, he was recognised by locals and overseas visitors alike. Some cheered and clapped him. Out came the cameras and Steve obliged by standing with groups of tourists who would be able to proudly go home and show their friends the moment when they met the famous Crocodile Hunter. But behind his usual smile for the cameras, he was concerned—the weather forecast was for overcast skies, which would do nothing for a documentary that would preferably show Queensland's typically blue skies and turquoise waters. Filming underwater would be a gloomy affair, too—but the deadlines that had to be met just could not wait.

He and his crew stood around a table in the main cabin discussing plans. They would head out to Agincourt Reef, some 40 miles north east of Port Douglas, and film whatever interested them. It was a loose schedule, but everyone was aware that with Steve Irwin starring anything could happen. His natural enthusiasm always spawned the unexpected …

On Sunday, 3 September, Steve found himself sitting in the aft section of a friend's vessel on the 18-kilometre (11-mile) long, 5-kilometre (3-mile) wide Batt Reef, lying 11 kilometres (6.5 miles) north of Port Douglas. The aluminium catamaran *Deepstar* was owned by 49-year-old underwater cameraman Pete West, whose underwater experience dates back to his teenage days at Marineland in Manly, a beachside suburb on Sydney's north shore.

As they sat together on the deck of the bobbing catamaran they chatted about their children—it was Father's Day and West was missing his ten-month-old daughter, Taylor. Steve admitted that he, too, wished he could have been with his family. Often his wife Terri and their children, Bindi, eight, and Bob, two, accompanied him on his outback adventures but this time they were on holiday in Tasmania.

'This is my first Father's Day,' West told him, 'and here I am miles away from home. My little girl is just wonderful, although she still hasn't learned to say "Dad",' said West.

'You're lucky, mate,' replied Steve. 'That's a lot better than me because I got called "mum, mum, mum", in the first month.' They both keeled over with laughter.

Inevitably, as they swallowed down soft drinks and ate snacks, the men's conversations turned to Steve's adventures and West asked how comfortable the Crocodile Hunter felt about working in what must seem like an alien environment, donning snorkelling gear to swim around a reef.

There were always risks, Steve responded—but West had a surprise up his sleeve.

'Look at this,' he said—and he laid out a kind of frogman's suit of armour, a stainless steel anti-shark chainmail outfit with a face helmet. The exclusive creation of a San Diego marine company, the suits are used by the company's own divers to swim in front of cages to entice sharks to attack them, so the action can be filmed by adventurers who are safe within the cages.

'The swarming sharks will often bite on the steel-suited divers, creating even more photo opportunities for you,' the company, Shark Diving Expeditions, enthuses in its sales pitch.

Anyway, that was how West described it to Steve, who stared in amazement at the custom-made suit that his friend had purchased for $7000.

'Crikey, how heavy is it, mate?' Steve asked his friend, reeling backwards in his typical showman style, blue eyes wide. Told it was 12 kilograms, he picked it up to feel the weight for himself.

No, he wouldn't be wearing one, he said, shaking his head. It wasn't his style. Steve Irwin had earned his reputation by getting up close and personal. He liked to approach his animal subjects as naturally as possible. In the raw without any protection. His sixth sense was his armoury, his defence. He liked to give his fans a sense of being with him when he crawled on his belly towards a large saltwater croc before leaping onto its back. Spectactors thrilled in anticipation that something unexpected might happen.

Taking risks was what made Steve such a crowd puller. His prerecorded wildlife documentaries featuring his confrontations with the world's deadliest creatures had won him a world-wide audience of more than 500 million. He was loved because he was genuine about what he did. His audience could feel it. Of course, there was the element of showmanship, the circus ringmaster, but in truth it was nature and its subjects—and the creatures that were often feared and loathed—that excited and enthralled him. He wanted to bring about a better understanding of those creatures which made people not only shudder, but in many cases hunt down and kill.

Looking at the chainmail suit and handling it, Steve told West he thought he would find wearing it too much of a burden despite the inclusion of a buoyancy vest. But Pete West was an enthusiast of the outfit and said he found it a real asset to his own cinematography business, National Underwater and Marine Agency, and in his view the money would have been well spent if it saved a life in Australian waters where many of the world's most dangerous creatures swam.

Unaware, of course, of what lay ahead for him in the next 24 hours, Steve listened casually to West's own risky adventures around the world, particularly when he was working on deep-sea oil rigs and also on expeditions for the military. While he was still flirting with danger by taking to waters alive with sharks, the steel-mesh suit would give him a better chance of staying alive to see his young daughter through her school years and into a career.

Back on board *Croc One*, Steve and the crew discussed the unpromising weather patterns and the continuing overcast skies which were frustrating their filming schedules. They had not been able to obtain the footage they had been hoping for. Terri and the children tried to call him to wish him a happy Father's Day, but unable to make contact with a voice call they had sent a text message, which was not picked up until the following day.

Croc One had returned to Batt Reef after filming on Agincourt Reef, where Steve swam among the colourful fish and picked up poisonous cone shells from the coral. He had hoped to track down and film a pair of giant, deadly stonefish that marine biologists said they had seen around the reef, but the search had been fruitless.

A local marine biologist had offered to show him a place on one of the outer reefs where the stonefish were known to live. 'I took a dive and for the first time in living memory they weren't there,' said the biologist. 'I couldn't believe it. If I found them, Steve would have concentrated on them ... '

There were few other marine creatures that would enhance the shoot. In any case, Steve was not excited about swimming around Agincourt, a reef that was easily accessible to the hundreds of tourists who travelled out there each day. There was the added disappointment of overcast skies and the effect they had of 'greying' the water and stifling the normally fluorescent colours of the reef dwellers.

'We should look around somewhere else,' Steve told *Croc One*'s skipper Chris Reed. So they sailed to Batt Reef where bull rays swam in large numbers, attracted by the abundance of shellfish on which they fed. There was an added plus: the shallow waters deterred the larger tourist vessels.

Over mugs of tea Steve animatedly recalled their previous day's filming of sea snakes but he wanted much more. They had had such a successful time in the Lakefield National Park that he wanted the Barrier Reef material to at least match it. He and John Stainton went on to chat about the deal they had signed with Disney and IMAX to make a 3D movie. Steve was hugely amused at the thought of himself a thousand times larger than life and seemingly jumping out of the screen with a crocodile in his arms.

Sometime during their discussions they agreed the bull rays would make a perfect sequence for his daughter Bindi's own children's show, which would be featured on the Animal Planet channel. Steve would be appearing with her. Action shots of him swimming among the rays could be exciting and different. The bigger the ray the better, of course, for in further discussions with his crew that night on board *Croc One*—moored about 1 kilometre (half a mile) north of *Deepstar* because its deeper draft prevented it from sailing close to the reef—they all agreed that the large, flat fish could save the day.

Their normally placid nature has earned them the title of 'the pussycats of the sea' and they have also been likened to an underwater magic carpet, gently flapping their 'wings' as they glide through the water. They are spectacular to watch.

But these pussycats of the sea have a sting in the tail—literally. They have three toxic-barbed spikes which can inflict excruciating pain and, in extreme circumstances, can kill. This defensive whip-like strike is used only in situations where the ray feels threatened or cornered, although the fish's first instinct is to escape by swimming away. The spikes, or spines, are pointed like spears and there are up to 40 tiny saw-like teeth on each edge, all coated with poison.

The result of one of these spines penetrating human flesh is unbearable pain and can also be fatal if the strike is to the heart of a swimmer who might accidentally brush against a ray as it 'glides' through its domain. The wound itself can become quickly infected while the injected poison causes severe pain and swelling. The force of the barb entering the body can be so powerful that it can easily sever a main artery. The victim could bleed to death before medical assistance arrives. An immediate treatment which claims to ease the pain and break down venom is to pour very hot water onto the wound. But in a severe attack, with a large amount of poison being injected, this can be ineffective.

While extremely rare, a number of stingray deaths are reported annually around the world. Victims of the stingray's toxic spike may also end up with their limbs amputated, so lethal is the poison.

Stingray Facts

- Growing to a width of 2 metres (6 feet) and a length of 4 metres (12 feet) rays are found in all the world's warm oceans, although some live in the rivers of South America.
- There are more than 150 types, bearing such names as the whiptail stingray, the estuary, bluntnose, thorntail, dragon, smalleye and leopard.
- Bottom dwellers with eyes set in the top of their head, they have an innocent-looking but powerful mouth underneath their flat bodies, which they use to suck up worms and crush clams and other shellfish foraged from the seabed.
- They are usually found in the shallows, where they lie partially buried in the sand or mud with only their eyes visible. Actually, they cannot see their prey, using instead a unique sense of smell and electro-receptors similar to those of the shark.
- Like sharks, stingrays give birth to live young, with three to five in a litter, and births can take place up to three times a year. Even the young carry a tiny tail spine with a small coating of poison.
- Stingrays have a unique way of keeping themselves spruced up, returning to what environmentalists have described as a 'cleaning station'—an area where reef fish tend to gather and eat the parasites on a ray's skin. The fish get a meal and the ray has a clean-up. Like humans, stingrays live alone, in pairs or in small groups.
- They are attractive to watch swimming and commercial divers have often filmed themselves swimming beside them—a risky hobby. As for those who have been hit by a stingray's barb, they have described the pain as excruciating, one American survivor saying the pain was like being stung by 1000 tarantulas.

On that fatal morning of Monday 4 September, Steve and his group had their final discussion on board *Croc One* about what they were going to film that day. As well as Steve, there were the two cameramen, Craig Lucas—a freelancer who had only recently completed an underwater course, but had been picked by Steve to help with the filming—and Justin Lyons, who had filmed Steve for many years; Philippe Cousteau, grandson of the famous ocean explorer Jacques Cousteau; Dr Jamie Seymour, a marine biologist from James Cook University; and John Stainton, Steve's long-time friend and manager who had 'discovered' him and introduced him to the world. Skipper Chris Reed was also there.

Justin Lyons gathered his camera equipment together as Steve prepared himself for the dive. They climbed into the white inflatable dinghy and Steve dived into the water. As an old mate, Justin was accustomed to Steve pushing the limits and getting into all kinds of scrapes.

Once, they had visited the Indonesian island of Flores to film the huge komodo dragons. These reptiles grow to 3 metres (12 feet) and can effortlessly bite through an arm or leg. Steve and the crew had a narrow escape, breaking a camera as they leaped out of harm's way when one of the dragons charged. Lyons recalled later: 'They're sort of placid, but they can turn very quickly.'

He was not to know how relevant those words would be when related to stingrays.

About half a kilometre away, Pete West stood on the deck of *Deepstar* with marine biologist and friend, Teresa Carrette, while two of his dive crew were in the water checking equipment and getting ready for the afternoon's filming. It was shortly after 11am. They watched the white inflatable dinghy from Steve's launch bobbing about several hundred metres away. They guessed he was just below somewhere, probably no more than 2 metres (6 feet) down, enjoying his swim with the rays. They hoped that Lyons and the second cameraman, Craig Lucas, who were down there with him, were getting some good footage.

As he continued going about his business on *Deepstar*, West paid no further attention to the dinghy—until, curiously, he heard its motor getting louder. The inflatable was racing towards *Deepstar*. Something was up.

Then Lyons was yelling up at West: 'It's Steve! He's been hit by a stingray!'

West stared down in horror. At Irwin lying face up and motionless on the floor of the dinghy beside Lyons' camera. A chill ran through West. There was a wound in Steve's chest—right over the heart. Blood was spreading rapidly. West quickly glanced towards *Croc One*. There was no indication that anyone on board was aware of what had happened.

West had some medical experience from his days working on oil rigs but he knew that the attention Steve Irwin required was far beyond his expertise. In their almost blind panic, the men filled the air with expletives. They were a long way from the urgent kind of medical help that Steve needed, but West believed he should be sped back to *Croc One* where the marine biologist Jamie Seymour might know what to do about such a terrible wound.

As Lyons turned the dinghy around and raced at full throttle to the distant launch, West grabbed the radio handset and hit the emergency VHF channel 16. Frustratingly, there was no response from the Port Douglas Coast Guard on that channel, so he tried calling up help from the next nearest coast guard station in Cairns, some 50 kilometres (31 miles) south of Port Douglas.

His voice was trembling as he made the call. It was 11.21am. 'Coast Guard Cairns! Coast Guard Cairns! This is *Deepstar*. We are in need of immediate medical assistance!'

He received an immediate response. West did not say who the victim was in that first exchange but on *Croc One* skipper Chris Reed heard the cry for help over his radio. Stainton and Reed dashed to the rear of the boat and saw the dinghy speeding towards them. They knew that something terrible had happened. Then they saw Steve lying in his blood on the floor of the dinghy.

The conservationist's limp body was hauled onto the back duck–board after Stainton had cut free a second dinghy moored there and which was in the way. Seymour examined Steve, but hope faded with every passing second.

On the radio to Cairns Coast Guard, Seymour switched to the closed channel 73, so he could discuss further urgent action without interruption from other vessels' skippers who would have picked up the initial distress call.

Seymour commandeered the radio. He knew how bad it was. He told the coastguard that an emergency evacuation was need. The crew felt like they were living through a nightmare. Steve, their friend, their workmate, was lying on the deck with what the feared was a fatal wound in his chest. He did not appear to be breathing. He was certainly not moving. They felt for a pulse and could find none. Yet there was not a man who was prepared to believe that Steve Irwin was dead. Someone tried the kiss of life. They tried kick-starting his heart with CPR to no avail. John Stainton told himself that Steve was dead, yet he would not, could not, say it to anyone, although he suspected that the others were now thinking the same thing.

There was one more desperate call to be made as, back on land an emergency helicopter was preparing to take off. Seymour called West on *Deepstar* and now West learned just how serious the incident was.

'Do you have a defibrillator there?' asked Seymour.

'Negative,' replied West. There were no heart-starters on his boat. 'Oxygen, yes, but sorry, no defibrillator.'

Now West knew from the question that Steve's heart had stopped. They were miles from anywhere. What hope did Steve Irwin have now?

Back on board *Croc One* there was no question of just spinning around and racing at full throttle towards Low Isles, halfway between Batt Reef and Port Douglas, where there was a heliport. The slightest mistake and *Croc One* would hit the reef—the coral had to be negotiated with great caution. As Reed worked his way through the reef and then opened up the throttle, the crew crowded around the still body of Steve Irwin, praying, cursing, hitting his chest, slapping his wrists. Terri was far away in Tasmania somewhere … what the hell were they going to tell her?

As *Croc One* headed away into the distance, West turned his own vessel towards the abandoned inflatable that Steve had been using. He recovered it and a second dinghy that had also been left behind. No-one on *Croc One* cared about dinghies at a time like this. The underwater camera was still lying in the dinghy. West brought it into the main cabin.

Lyons called up on the radio, concerned about the camera he had abandoned on the dinghy. *Croc One* had arrived at Low Isles at 11.50 am. The emergency helicopter team touched down only 10 minutes later.

West assured Lyons he had recovered the camera..

'How's Steve doing?' West then asked.

There was a moment's silence before Lyons replied: 'He's in the hands of professionals.'

Then he continued: 'The camera … can you make sure it's secure and also ensure the tape isn't stuffed. It's vital.'

West, familiar with the equipment, pressed the playback button.

He and Teresa Carrette watched the last few seconds on the small viewfinder and were shocked at what they saw. There was a 2.5-metre (8-foot) ray, with Steve swimming above. They were about to watch a man die. West was to describe later how he saw graphic footage in a medium to wide shot as the ray suddenly whipped up its deadly tail and struck Steve in the chest with a barb. He knew then that Steve Irwin had no chance of survival. In that fatal moment Irwin instinctively grabbed the barb and tore it from his chest. It was the last move the Crocodile Hunter would make.

The effort to keep him alive had been frantic. When *Croc One* reached Low Isles, with the rescue helicopter still on the way, the crew of a charter boat *Wave Dancer*, owned by dive company Quicksilver, also tried to revive him, this time with a defibrillator, without success.

Enid Traill, a nurse who was on holiday, was taking a stroll around the island, mingling with some 50 other tourists enjoying a sightseeing or diving day out, when she heard someone counting … 'one … two … three … !' Instinctively she knew what that meant. A medical emergency. Someone's heart being pumped.

Moments later, she saw a group of men carrying someone up the beach. It was a confusing scene, for there was a camera crew there, too. She thought perhaps that it had just been a movie or a documentary, after all. But the faces of the men were grim. It was too real. The holder of advanced resuscitation qualifications, she hurried over.

'Can I help … I'm a nurse?'

Heads nodded frantically. They carried the limp figure into a boat shed, Mrs Traill still unaware of who the man was. The daughter of the late Jack Spender, known as 'Mr Lifesaving' in Queensland after setting up the association's state headquarters, 55-year-old Mrs Traill took over the CPR. 'I knew it was a terrible situation because we couldn't get any air into his lungs,' she recalled later. 'We tried and tried for ten minutes or so, but it was all to no avail.'

The paramedics arrived on a Careflight helicopter from Queensland Helicopter Rescue. The medical team also had no idea who the victim was. As they took over from Mrs Traill, she watched helplessly as they 'examined the hole in his heart.' One of the paramedics asked: 'Have we got an ID on this man?'

John Stainton stepped forward. 'It's Steve Irwin,' he said.

There was a moment's silence. 'Are we talking about the Steve Irwin?' the paramedic asked.

'Yes,' said John.

Mrs Traill looked to the medical team in shock. It was a terrible moment, one she would never forget, for, curiously, she had known Steve as a teenager when he would call at her family's marine refrigeration business in Caloundra to see one of the apprentices who worked there. 'The fact that he was from "home" and someone I knew made the impact greater on me. I would rather say I wasn't there, but I was.'

She remembered how he would turn up at the workshop with lizards in his pockets and how, in recent years, he would help to support fundraising activities for the Dicky Beach surf club that Mrs Traill is still associated with.

Despite the efforts of everyone, on *Croc One*, on the shore of the island and in the boat shed, the conclusion was reached that Steve Irwin was beyond all help. He was pronounced dead at 12.53pm, some one and a half hours after he had received that fatal strike.

'They told me he wouldn't have survived even if he'd received that wound in an operating theatre and there was medical help available on the spot,' Mrs Traill said.

Careflight doctor Ed O'Loughlin confirmed the hopelessness.

'It became clear fairly soon he had non-survivable injuries,' he said.

Steve's body was flown to the mainland and then transported to the mortuary at Cairns Hospital.

Could he have been saved if he had not torn the spike from his chest?

It seemed unlikely, but in any case medical experts and marine specialists agreed that his instinctive reaction to rip it out before he lapsed into unconsciousness would have increased the damage. Having already been struck in the heart, like a man being hit by a barbed arrow, jerking it out would have resulted in added tearing. Marine specialist Peter Fenner was convinced that the action would have made matters much worse—'the more you start pulling things around, the more damage you do to yourself,' he said as the shock news spread around the world.

A scientist at the Australian Venom Research Unit at Melbourne University, Dr Bryan Fry, believed that leaving the barb in the chest would have stemmed the bleeding, whereas pulling it out would have taken a lot of force and would possibly have caused more damage. The serrations, he said, meant the spike would not slide out like a knife.

Generally, said a surgeon, Hugh Wolfenden, who works at the Prince of Wales Hospital in Sydney, it would not be advisable to remove an object because while still in place it helps to stem the bleeding. On the other hand, leaving it in the heart could also be problematical if the heart was still beating because the action of the heart could result in it lacerating itself against the foreign object.

As for the poison, experts were divided on whether it would have killed Steve. Geoff Isbister, a clinical toxicologist based at Newcastle's Mater Hospital, north of Sydney, believed that although the venom might have caused tissue damage, the physical trauma to Steve would have been enough to end his life.

It had been an early spring day in Australia, but that afternoon a chill had settled on the entire country; a chill that spread around the globe like a fast-moving frost.

3

Crocs Rule!

Fear is a natural thing that us humans have. It keeps us alive. So every time I go in on a venomous snake, a crocodile, a bear, a cougar, a tiger shark—any wild animal—I get a little scared, a little nervy.
Fear is a good thing.

As the mind-numbing hours slipped by, a shocked and grief-stricken John Stainton bravely faced the cameras to speak of Steve Irwin's final tragic moments. It was, he said, the worst day of his life. He did not reveal at that time the desperate attempts that had been made to try to reach Terri and pass on the terrible news.

Instead, as he spoke of the tragedy, he said the pain of losing his friend had been worsened when he thought about all the places they had been together, all the adventures, the documentaries they had made and the dangerous situations they had overcome.

It was hard to accept that the man who was so much a part of his life was gone.

On so many occasions, he said, during their long association, he had forced Steve to do interviews against his wishes. But now John said he felt it was only right that he step up to the responsibility of facing the world's media in spite of his own sorrow.

Yes, of course, on many occasions they had discussed the risks Steve had taken as he leaped away from the snapping jaws of man-eating crocodiles and ducked the lightning strike of poisonous snakes. Until that fatal day he had always been able to anticipate their next move and sidestep danger.

'If ever he was going to go, we always said it was going to be the ocean, because there you have another element from the land he was so accustomed to,' said John. 'On land, he was agile, quick-thinking, quick-moving. The ocean puts another element there that you have no control over. We'd talked about death and its likelihood on occasions over the years but Steve always brushed the thought of his own death aside.

'It just came with the territory,' was something he'd always say. There's been a million occasions where both of us held our breath and thought we were lucky to get out of that one. But Steve, you know, just seemed to have a charmed life. He certainly wasn't worried about the rays.'

Tears rolled down John Stainton's cheeks as he struggled to find words to describe what had happened to his friend in those shallow waters. 'I don't think he would have felt any pain,' he said. 'It was a very unfortunate accident the way it happened. He came over the top of the ray and the barb came up.

'The cameraman said he didn't know that it had even hit him until he saw blood in the water and then he knew there was a problem. He swam over to him and helped him up to the surface.

'We got him back within a couple of minutes to *Croc One* and we tried to quickly trip back to Low Isles, where we were going to meet the emergency rescue people to do immediate and constant CPR, try and resuscitate him back into life. When we got there it was probably 10 minutes to 12 noon and by 12 o'clock, when the emergency crew arrived, they pronounced him dead.

'Steve left this world doing what he loved doing best. He left this world in a happy and peaceful state of mind. He would have said: "Crocs Rule".'

John Stainton hesitated, overcome. Then he continued: 'There's so many things that were going to happen, you know—just gone now.'

But what exactly had happened down there? 'It was shocking.' He had watched the video after Steve West, from the *Deepstar*, had handed the camera over to the crew.

'It's a very hard thing to watch because you're actually witnessing somebody die … and it's terrible. It shows that Steve came over the top of the ray and the tail came up and spiked him here'—he pointed to his chest—'and he pulled it out and the next minute he's gone. That was it. The cameraman had to shut down. I think—and the coroner's report will say what happened—but I think he died fairly instantly.'

He shook his head as he returned to the freak underwater accident that had ended the Crocodile Hunter's life. 'I think we all had that belief that we'd pull through whatever situation we were in and he has been in some very close shaves with snakes and crocodiles. I would never imagine it to come from something like a stingray.'

The tape of Steve's last moments was so harrowing, he said, that it should never be revealed to the public. It should be destroyed to ensure that no-one got their hands on it and found a way of publishing it. 'As far as I'm concerned, it's never going to see the light of day,' he said.

He had already handed it over to Queensland police who would, in turn, pass it to the Queensland coroner if an inquest was held. Although senior police officers said there were no suspicious circumstances surrounding Steve's death, it was suggested an inquest might still be held because of the unusual way he had died.

But his fans and close friends were holding their own mini-inquests around the world. Had Steve made a terrible mistake—or was his death an accident that could not have been avoided? Having tackled man-eating crocodiles, handled the most dangerous snakes in the world, did he believe he was invincible? Had he slipped into 'automatic', just getting as close to the subject of his filming without thinking about the consequences to himself? The questions, which the coroner would be likely to ask, went on but there was one more: had he burned himself out over the years, done so much damage to his body, that his reflexes weren't as quick as they used to be? He was approaching his mid-40s and he'd bashed himself about more than a first-grade rugby player or a boxer.

There were clues to his fitness in an interview he had with top Australian interviewer Andrew Denton on *Enough Rope* in March 2004. His knee, he said was 'buggered', adding: 'I haven't surfed for like six months now and got told I'll probably never surf again, which dealt a devastating blow, you know. I'm a mad surfer. But I've run out of cartilage and now it's bone on bone and this is the first day that I've actually been able to walk after just about a week of no walking.

'So, you know, it's taken its toll it really has. It really, really has. My knee … I've got two broken ribs at the moment, and my finger can't straighten. I snapped it. I caught this croc and he attacked me and broke it off and [there are] blood bits and pieces starting to go now … you know what I'm not, I'm not bouncing … I'm not bouncing back like I used to Andy. It's just, you know it's taken it's toll. Yeah, but such is life.'

His confession about his breaking down body was not something to be discussed by John Stainton in the hours after Steve's death. All that mattered to the sandy-haired film-maker at that time was that his great friend was no more.

They had made a great team, Stainton and Steve. A slick, wildlife marketing machine that penetrated far corners of the world. It says much for John Stainton's stoicism to understand that in those terrible days that followed Steve's death he had shown himself to be a true professional and a friend that anyone would be proud of. Inundated with calls from fans and the media, he had handled all that was humanly possible, going without sleep for 60 hours and retaining his dignity. Although he had plenty of offers to help with the incessant calls and inquiries, he remained determined to handle them personally because he believed that beyond Steve's immediate family, he knew the conservationist better than anyone.

Their extraordinary relationship had started when Steve, aware of John Stainton's brilliant career as an award-winning film-maker—he has been behind dozens of top-rating documentaries—handed over a stack of videos that Steve had starred in and filmed himself. They showed a bug-eyed bush larrikin engaged in desperate wrestling bouts with massive crocodiles.

Bob Irwin, Steve's father, sick of the ribbing his mates gave him when he told them of his son's prowess in capturing crocs, had given Steve an old National video camera to capture his exploits on film. The camera was going to shut them up. All the proof was there. These were tapes that Steve handed to John Stainton and started a relationship that was to go on for 20 years. John Stainton found Steve Irwin's homestyle 'Crocodile Dundee' movies hugely amusing and, oddly, instructive.

Not only was his enthusiasm infectious, but his real affection for his man-eating co-stars was riveting.

The canny producer could recognise natural screen presence. Steve's amateur efforts showed he had it in abundance. From that moment, a friendship and partnership was forged between the city slicker and the nature-loving boy from the bush.

John's judgement was spot on, but then he did have the experience of more than 30 years in the Australian television and film industry, winning the country's Penguin Award for Best Documentary for his film on the Sahara Desert, *Journey to a Legend*.

At that time Steve had already embarked on his dream of helping his parents give their wildlife park a higher profile, and the early traces of the eco-warrior he was to become had begun to emerge.

When Steve met Terri and asked her to marry him it seemed perfectly natural that they should take the next step on that dream together. As is now famously known, their honeymoon in 1992 was spent chasing crocodiles for the first episode of *The Crocodile Hunter* series, created in conjunction with John Stainton. The episodes were shown on Animal Planet and the star, Steve Irwin, was an overnight sensation. The United States could not get enough of him. His every adventure was breathlessly followed.

The success of the series was astounding. Before his own country, Australia, took him to its heart he was a megastar. So big, in fact, that in time John Stainton considered moving Steve from the small screen to the big screen—a Hollywood-style movie with Steve and Terri starring as themselves and which would still drive home their environmental message.

'I didn't want to blast into the movies with a make-believe, shoot-em-up style of film,' Stainton was to say in an interview. 'I felt we had to approach it carefully so that we kept Steve as a true and honest man. He shouldn't play another character. He shouldn't be acting. He had to do what he does in real life and he had to do the things he was comfortable with.'

Eventually for that feature movie he decided to film Steve just as he'd always done, taking him into the outback and allowing him to show his crocodile-catching skills while actors played out a sub-plot. But John was determined that Steve would not become just a celluloid hero. He had already proved himself on the small screen as himself, a true and honest man with a passion for his environment and the animals that lived in it. A generous man who included all those around him in his success and who loved his friends and family unconditionally.

As he wept for the loss of his dear friend, it seemed to John as though he had lost his right arm—or even a piece of his heart. As he contemplated a future without Steve he saw only a great void. Yet he had no doubt that Steve's work would continue. The star attraction was gone but he was so loved that the devoted team behind him would carry on, and be carried along, by the impetus of what had been created by his Crocodile Hunter persona.

What was hard for him to listen to was wild speculation that Steve had provoked the stingray in some way, perhaps hoping to show viewers how it could flick up its tail when attacked by a predator. Such gossip was quickly dismissed, not only by John Stainton but by the man Steve had talked to shortly before his death.

'Under no circumstances,' said Peter West, from the *Deepstar*, who had also viewed the videotape showing Steve's encounter with the stingway, 'was he harassing the animal. He wasn't poking or prodding it at all. The rest was just a tragedy. He was just doing what he normally does.'

Famous Australian marine documentary maker Ben Cropp, who in 2004 was attacked by a tiger shark on Bott Reef, had been diving on the Great Barrier Reef at the time of the stingray attack and, although he was not at the scene of the incident, he soon learned from a crew member what had happened.

'In this case, he was swimming alongside a bull ray, a big black ray, and the cameraman would have been in front, filming him,' said Cropp. 'Steve got maybe a bit too close to the ray and with the cameraman in front the ray must have felt sort of cornered. It went into a defensive mode, stopped, turned around and lashed out with its tail, which has a considerable spike on it. Unfortunately, Steve was directly in its path and he took a fatal wound.

'I have had that happen to me and I can visualise it—when a ray goes into defensive, you get out of the way. Steve was so close he could not get away, so if you can imagine it … being right beside the ray and it swinging its spine upwards from underneath Steve … and it hit him. I have seen that sort of reaction with rays, with their tail breaking the water, such is the force.'

Such was the force of Irwin's presence on the world stage that news network websites were paralysed as details of his death flashed around the world. The demand for information in Australia was so great that the Australian Broadcasting Commission had to strip graphics from its website and offer a low-bandwidth version.

'We've not had anything like this for a very long time,' said the acting head of the network's IT department Craig Preston. Traffic levels were higher than those that came in the wake of the London bombings in July 2005. Whereas important current affairs stories receive around 25,000 hits on Australia's News Interactive website, coverage of Steve Irwin's death had received half a million. More than 2000 comments and tributes were posted by site visitors in less than four hours, while videos linked to the story received 40,000 hits.

All other news took second place. High profile anchormen and anchorwomen of the major networks, Hollywood stars, world leaders—they were all horrified by the news. Steve Irwin had appeared as himself alongside Eddie Murphy in the movie *Doctor Dolittle 2* and had been a guest on Larry King Live, the *Tonight Show* with Jay Leno and the *Rosie O'Donnell Show*. Pictures of Steve wrestling crocodiles, tramping through mosquito-infested creeks and dangling deadly snakes in his hands had graced thousands of global magazines and newspapers.

In Australia's Federal Parliament in Canberra, proceedings came to a grinding halt. As commentator Matt Price was to recall later, 'it was such an eerie afternoon.' In the middle of paying its respects to the death of Australian Democrats founder Don Chipp, word began to filter into the chamber that Steve Irwin had died. What was thought to have been nothing more than a rumour at the time had come from Families, Community Services and Indigenous Affairs Minister Mal Brough, but by the time Prime Minister John Howard had finished paying tribute to Mr Chipp, Steve Irwin's death had been confirmed.

Mr Brough was deeply distressed—he lives a few kilometres from Steve's Australia Zoo north of Brisbane and the two families had become close friends. In fact, the minister's children work part-time at the zoo, and Steve was a significant employer and generous donor in Mr Brough's seat. Until the entire chamber realised why he was so upset, opposition MPs had decided to go on the attack when they noticed Mr Brough's demeanour.

'Gee, I hope we're not asking Mal a question,' said one Labor MP. 'It looks like something dreadful has happened to him.'

But it wasn't just the minister who was upset. John Howard, once described by Steve as 'the greatest leader Australia has ever had and the greatest leader in the world,' was also visibly shaken.

Soon, word of the disaster in northern Queensland was spreading through the back benches and into the press gallery. MPs refrained from public comment, however, for they were concerned that Steve's wife—no-one could even think of her as a widow—had not been informed of his death.

But once it had been confirmed by Queensland police and Mr Howard had viewed first details of Steve's death on a staff member's laptop computer, the Prime Minister said outside the House: 'He was a character for lots of people around the world, a wonderful character. His is a huge loss to Australia. He was a passionate environmentalist. He brought joy and entertainment and excitement to millions of people.' Such was the emotion that Mr Howard felt, he indicated he would offer the conservationist's family a state funeral if they wished it.

It was Mr Howard who had arranged an extraordinary barbecue at his official residence, the Lodge, in Canberra on 23 October 2003. There were three very special guests of honour. One was George W. Bush, President of the United States, the most powerful man in the world.

The other two were Steve and Terri Irwin. Other guests included tennis star Lleyton Hewitt, Mr Howard's sons Tim and Richard and other VIPs, including Michael Thawley, then Australian Ambassador to Washington, and Mr Peter Varghese, the upcoming head of the Office of National Assessments. Everyone wore suits and ties for the marquee barbecue but two people stood out among the formal attire—Brigadier Maurie McNairn, head of the Australian forces in the Iraq invasion was there in full khaki uniform, and Steve in his trademark bush garb. Terri would no doubt have also turned up in a safari gear, but she was heavily pregnant at the time with baby Bob, so a black maternity dress was more comfortable.

President Bush made it known that he was a great fan of Steve, even if he didn't say so in so many words. But his body language was enough. He wandered over to the wildlife warrior and, as political columnist Malcolm Farr was to observe later after watching them hold an animated conversation, 'it was almost like a meeting of equals—America's top wildlife celebrity meets its commander in chief.' Farr noted that they got on well, even though 'the bushman stayed seated as he spoke to Bush.'

One day later, Greens Senator Bob Brown, who might have expected some support from Steve, interrupted Bush's speech to Parliament. This infuriated Steve. 'Oh crikey, mate,' he said when asked what he thought about Brown, 'he needs to taken out the back and given a good belting.'

What had cemented the relationship between Mr Howard and Steve had been the conservationist's invitation to Mr Howard to formally open the refurbished Australia Zoo 20 days before the Bush barbecue. Mr Howard had been welcomed by Bindi, then aged five. Looking up at him and with a child's lack of guile, she had said: 'Prime Minister, we're glad you run the country.'

Then it had been Steve's turn to take over at that event in Queensland, embarrassing Mr Howard by declaring him to be the greatest leader Australia had ever had and the 'greatest leader in the entire world. I get to meet some extraordinary people and extraordinary leaders, but meeting the Prime Minister is the proudest moment of my life.'

'No wonder he was invited to the barbie,' Farr noted.

In that same year a different sort of menu was being suggested for a different kind of political lunch. Queensland Premier Peter Beattie said he was considering crocodile for the menu at the Commonwealth Heads of Government Meeting that was to be held in Brisbane the following month and he planned to have Steve among the hand-picked celebrities welcoming the dignitaries.

Steve was incensed. 'I think Peter Beattie is a total dickhead to ask Steve Irwin, the Crocodile Hunter, to come and eat crocodile. It's like asking a dog lover to come along and eat dog satay.'

As it transpired, the delegates were not served crocodile and if Peter Beattie was offended by the dickhead remark, he appeared to have forgotten all about it a few months later when he announced that Steve had been appointed an honourary ambassador for Queensland.

'He's one of the best exports Queensland has had and he's on a par with Greg Norman.'

4

If It Thinks You're Afraid,
It Will Have You for Dinner

Yeah, I'm a thrill seeker, but crikey,
education's the most important thing.

Steve had shown that he could easily mix with anybody—everyday visitors to his zoo, world leaders and film stars. He was the same man with all of them.

On his death, his friend, actor Russell Crowe, said he was 'the Australian that we all aspire to.' Speaking in New York, the Oscar winning actor added: 'He held an absolute belief about caring for the riches of our country, meaning specifically that the riches of our fauna was the highest priority we should have. Over time we might just see how right he was. He was, and remains, the ultimate wildlife warrior. He touched my heart. I believed in him. I'll miss him. I loved him and I'll be there for his family.'

Crowe's tribute was directed towards a star as great as his own standing on the world stage, particularly in the United States. The

Crocodile Hunter had such star power that when he travelled to America he needed heavy security to keep fans at bay during his tours and he often had to resort to moving about in disguise. No wonder the whole world reacted when he was lost to them.

The floodgates were open. News of Steve's death travelled so fast that it hit the website of American television network CBS even before some Australian news sites.

From the al-Jazeera network in Asia to television stations in South Africa, India, Europe and South America, the name of Steve Irwin was pronounced in numerous accents. American drawl on Fox television and precise Queen's English on the BBC—many tongues and dialects carried the same message, that the Crocodile Hunter, the Crocodile Man, the Wildlife Warrior, call him what they would, was no longer with them. Headlines blared out words that told of his 'freak death', some bade him farewell, while journalists who had met Steve or interviewed him over crackly telephone lines, talk show hosts who had sat with him in front of their cameras, and ordinary people all claimed to have shared his presence either in person or by watching his documentaries in their sitting rooms.

Proudly, I joined them. It was impossible to have spoken to him without having a lasting memory. What did I think of him? Of course he was a showman—I knew that before I travelled up to his Australia Zoo to interview him and Terri shortly after the birth of their first child, Bindi. He'd announced not long before that he planned to raise Bindi with animals all around her so that not only would she show no fear of them later in life, but she would also come to understand that they should be respected and, above all, to never forget that those which lived in the wild were, indeed, wild animals whose behaviour was unpredictable. How did he intend to get that message across to such a tiny child? Easy, of course—he was going to introduce her to a huge python that lived in the zoo.

So, in 1988, I travelled from Sydney to Beerwah, an hour or so's drive from Brisbane where the Australia Zoo is located, set back off a tree-lined road near the resort town of Caloundra. Steve emerged from their private quarters with Terri, both in their trademark khaki outfits. He was bubbly, bright and almost child-like in his enthusiasm for his animal world. She was quieter, but charmingly so.

We spoke of his own childhood and how he had been brought up by his parents. Bob and Lyn Irwin had run the small reptile and fauna park in those very grounds in which we now stood and they had instilled in him his appreciation of the environment. He related how he had met Terri when she visited the zoo and how he planned to devote the rest of his life to conservation. During our chat, Terri excused herself, to return with baby Bindi in her arms.

We discussed the story I wanted to write: how he had been teaching Bindi about wild animals, just as his parents had taught him. 'Well, come on then,' he said. 'Let's do it'—and then he was hurrying ahead down a path towards an enclosure where, minutes later, he was holding a massive python in his arms.

'That's a big snake,' I said, stepping back nervously. 'And it looks pretty heavy, too.'

'It is that, mate,' he said. 'Here, try it on.' Before I could move away even further he had draped the monster reptile around my neck. 'Don't let it think you're afraid,' he said with a huge grin. 'If it thinks you're afraid of it, it will have you for dinner.'

He was joking. Or at least I hoped he was. In any case, he finally relieved me of it and then, taking Bindi from Terri, held the little girl in one arm as he held the snake in the other. Then he struck an amazing pose, freezing like a statue, the snake's head against Bindi's face as he stared, eyes popping in mock amazement, into my camera. It was a pose I was to see repeated many times over the years, but that was Steve. He loved the camera and, it must be said, the camera loved him.

But what of his voice? That Aussie twang and those 'ocker' expressions … people, myself included, had wondered if that was all for the television cameras. But no, that was truly Steve on and off the world stage. What you saw on television was just how he was. More of my meeting with Steve Irwin and his zoo later, for it would be too soon here to leave the tributes that poured in from around the world in the wake of his untimely death.

As the flowers piled up at the gates of the Australia Zoo and people stood weeping, newspaper letters columns around the globe bulged with tributes. Australians abroad became suddenly fiercely patriotic, proudly revealing or confirming that they were from the same country as Steve Irwin.

'Living abroad for five years,' wrote Michelle Cummins, 'I lost count of the number of times people yelled "Crikey!" or "Look at this beauty!" as soon as they found out that I was an Australian. My knee-jerk reaction was to cringe, so I was surprised to find myself so very deeply saddened by the death of Steve Irwin. His exuberance could sometimes border on annoying, but I see now it was a result of his passion. He was a family man who loved nature's creatures more than he feared them and I now find myself wondering why I wasted so much time explaining to foreigners that not all Australians are like him. Goodness knows, the world would be a better place if more of us were like him.'

It was clear from that first flood of letters that people who knew nothing more about the man than the exuberant personality they had seen on television believed it would be difficult, if not impossible, to replace him.

'I did not know Steve Irwin, but he epitomised the larrikin Aussie and everything good about our country,' wrote Beverley Rogerson from Rainbow Flat. 'What a great ambassador, who tried to promote Australia and did so quite successfully around the world. I wish that we had someone to take his place. What a huge role to fill.'

Such was the theme that continued without pause. 'It is not often that a passionate, energetic man stands out in the world of ordinary people and it is interesting to see how Steve Irwin was embraced worldwide,' wrote Samantha Shaw of Sydney. 'Overseas, he was a hero. To children and people with imagination and a love for the outdoors, he was a hero. But typically, he was the first to be criticised and frowned on by a lot of Australians. Now that he's gone and the country realises what a ray of light he shone, and what a difference he made, I hope those who cringed at his style realise that it is those out-of-the-ordinary people who make the world go round.'

'Steve Irwin as the posthumous Australian of the Year—what greater tribute could we give?' asked Sandra Simpson, also of Sydney. Echoing thoughts about whether he could ever be replaced, Geoff Purssell noted that Steve Irwin 'has left us with a legacy in regard to his passion and dedication to the animal kingdom. I for one can only admire his sense of fun and adventure. I sincerely doubt we will see such a character again.'

But it was not just Australians who spoke passionately about the loss of the man and his work.

From Spokane, Washington, Melissa Coggin declared that Steve did more for animal conservation than any person she knew, describing him as a 'superb human being.' She added: 'If he were from my country, I would be grateful to him for everything he gave of himself so willingly. Shame on anyone who thought of him as an embarrassment. He will be dearly missed here in America.'

Another American, David R Caine, ironically from San Diego, California, where the steel-mesh dive suit that Steve examined shortly before his death was made, said that the conservationist lived the life that he and his friends dreamed of 'and we came to love him for his passion and dedication to the environment.'

In the tiny Pacific island nation of Vanuatu, Steve and his team had helped capture and return a rogue estuarine crocodile to its home in one of the northern islands in the group. On hearing that he had been killed by a stingray, the indigenous people who had helped in the exercise wept.

In Thailand a group of elephant trainers set up a shrine to Steve at an elephant camp in Ayutthaya, north of Bangkok. During a memorial service, surrounded by a number of their elephants, the trainers gazed at a large photograph of Steve clutching a crocodile over the caption: 'Died doing what he loved.' John Stainton had revealed that Steve was not only passionate about reptiles, he simply adored elephants and had pledged more than $A30,000 to a DNA project for Thai elephants. He was due to visit the camp in the following month of October to make a documentary about their lives.

The DNA money was an example of Steve's 'behind the screen' generosity, for the profits he made from his television shows as the Crocodile Hunter were destined to be poured back into many conservation projects at home and abroad.

If he heard that a particular species was in danger he would buy up land nearby to help with the preservation of the animals or birds. Steve had a plan to turn large areas of land into havens for wildlife—his own kind of national parks.

'Whenever we get enough cash and a chunk of land that we're passionate about, bang, we buy it,' he said in an interview with Australian talk show host Andrew Denton, on *Enough Rope* in 2003. 'What we're trying to do is we're trying to set an example to the world that every single person can make a difference—particularly those in the political arena, those that have zoological facilities, any, you know, multinationals, any millionaires. They can make a difference by buying chunks of land.'

His enthusiasm won applause from the Australian Wildlife Conservancy, which buys or acquires land for conservation. After Steve's death, Atticus Fleming, chief executive of the organisation which claims to protect 250 ecosystems, 100 threatened ecosystems and 135 threatened animal species, praised Steve for the environmental legacy he had left behind.

'We were both looking to do the same thing,' he recalled. 'We sat down and had a beer and talked about how we might do that better, and how we might help each other.'

Steve, of course, caught the world's attention with his showmanship. In his homeland he was almost a caricature of all that was mocked and derided in a traditional Aussie male. But not in America and the 136 countries into which his documentaries were beamed. His 'Crikey!' catchphrase and astonishing exploits with savage and poisonous animals thrilled his audience who wanted more and more. While his message to save the environment came through loud and clear, there were some who believed he was far too much of a showman to be ever taken seriously. The chorus of criticism was led by none other than fellow Australian and feminist Germaine Greer, now a resident of London.

'What Irwin failed to understand,' she wrote in a savage attack in *The Guardian* newspaper, 'was that animals need space. The one lesson any conservationist must labour to drive home is that habitat loss is the principal cause of species loss. There was no habitat, no matter how fragile or finely balanced, that Irwin hesitated to barge into, trumpeting his wonder and amazement to the skies. There was not an animal he was not prepared to manhandle. Every creature he brandished at the camera was in distress. Every snake badgered by Irwin was at a huge disadvantage, with only a single possible reaction to its terrifying situation, which was to strike.'

In what was condemned as a cruel and unnecessary farewell message from a woman who had once been so admired by her compatriots for her fight for women's rights, Miss Greer concluded: 'The animal world has finally taken its revenge on Irwin, but probably not before a whole generation of kids in shorts seven sizes too small has learned to shout in the ears of animals with hearing 10 times more acute than theirs, determined to become millionaire animal-loving zoo-owners in their turn.'

She followed up her written remarks later by reportedly saying that those who mourned Irwin were 'idiots'. The British maligned them, she said, as having a 'Princess Diana moment.' She added that she did not understand Australians' sense of loss for Irwin, suggesting that the 'whole Steve Irwin phenomenon' was embarrassing.

Reaction was swift. Angry Australian leaders told Miss Greer to shut up—'I think Germaine Greer should just stick a sock in it,' said Labor foreign affairs spokesman Kevin Rudd. Sydney's *Daily Telegraph* said it was preparing a Dr Hannibal Lecter-style mask to send to Miss Greer to keep her quiet. Yet she was not alone with her sentiments.

Similar thoughts were expressed by others compelled to air their condemnation of Steve's methods in the newspapers. 'Steve Irwin spent his life irritating animals … Karma,' wrote Jen Lynch from Sydney's Camperdown.

There was, too, a sideswipe from Mark Goddard of Sydney's Pyrmont. 'How will we ever replace Steve Irwin? It won't be easy to find somebody to represent Australia to the world as a nation of khaki-clad, jabbering idiots with a penchant for feeding a crocodile with one hand while holding their infant son in the other. Yes, big shoes to fill indeed.'

Steve's death was seen as an opportunity by many who disagreed with his style to come out on the attack. Little notice might have been taken of them while the conservationist was alive, but his death had opened the gates for every kind of opinion. The pro-animal organisation People for the Ethical Treatment of Animals (PETA) said it was not shocked to learn that Steve Irwin had died 'provoking a dangerous animal.'

There had been no evidence that Steve had annoyed the stingray—on the contrary—but PETA activist Dan Matthews was not prepared to go soft on the Crocodile Hunter. 'He made a career out of antagonising frightened animals, which is a dangerous message to send to kids,' he said. 'If you compare him with a responsible conservationist like Jacques Cousteau, he looks like a cheap reality television star.'

Matthews' comments were posted on the Internet, provoking a wave of protest. But PETA came back with a statement by spokeswoman Lisa Wothne who said it was inevitable that Steve Irwin would meet his death with an animal. 'He liked to portray himself as for wildlife, but the truth is he exploited animals for entertainment. The whole premise of his show was based on harassing wildlife.'

There were a lot of people who did not think so. At the zoo gates the bouquets of flowers, messages of sympathy and other outpourings of grief continued to mount, reminding many of the crowds who came to pay their respects to Princess Diana at Kensington Palace following her death in a car crash. Australia Zoo is located on the Sunshine Coast hinterland, reachable only by car or bus, but even so the crowds found their way there somehow and tearfully placed their tributes all against the perimeter walls. Children laid down personally drawn cards of respect, with drawings of sharks and crocodiles. The mourning was overwhelming, like nothing Australia had witnessed in its entire history.

'To the Crocodile Hunter,' wrote one child, Logan. 'I'm very sorry for you dieing [sic] yesterday. You were cool. I like you.'

Somebody left a toy crocodile there while 'Terry' dropped a suede desert boot at the door with a message in black ink scrawled across the top: 'Steve, I take my shoe off for you, mate.'

Five-year-old Kai Hardge, from Sydney, wrote a letter to God: 'Steve Irwin was a wonderful man because he could deal with poisonous animals like snakes and animals that were not poisonous like crocodiles.'

They poured in from numerous countries, those messages of farewell and condolence. 'Steve rulz,' blared out an inscription on a T-shirt. There at the zoo entrance was Dwayne Brackhahn, 61, and his 22-year-old son Ty, of Portland, USA, who were on holiday in Queensland when they heard of Steve's death. 'We came to pay our respects to a guy that brought so much happiness to Americans,' said Mr Brackhahn.

As usual, mindful that Steve would want the show to go on, the zoo opened its gates on time the day after his death. 'He would have kicked our butts today if it wasn't opened,' media manager Louise Martin said.

I'd met Louise some months earlier when she'd taken me around to the pen of Harriet the Galapagos tortoise. I had gone to the zoo to write a story about Harriet's 175th birthday. Steve was away on an outback expedition but Louise told me that Harriet was one of his prized 'boarders'. 'Steve must be doing something right in looking after her,' she said at the time. 'Harriet is breaking all the records for long life.'

At the zoo gates was another staff member, Amber Gillett. I'd also met her previously. She wept openly as she placed a letter to her departed boss at a small shrine of flowers. 'We promise, I promise, to carry your legacy around the world as you envisioned,' she wrote. 'We will miss your happy face so much!!'

But would the zoo be able to carry on without its much-loved 'head keeper'?

'There is no question about that,' said Miss Martin, explaining that work on a $A40 million expansion plan would continue. Steve had been looking forward to the opening at Christmas of a new elephant enclosure that he had helped design and partially built. 'It's something he definitely would have looked forward to and then we have another of our features, Madagascar Island, happening. He'd been out on his bulldozer digging away because he loved that and all his "boy's toys".'

Zoo spokesman Peter Lang, revealing that a World Wildlife Warriors Steve Irwin Memorial Fund would be set up, said: 'He touched people all around the world. He was far more than just a character in khaki.'

Unexpectedly Steve's dad, Bob Irwin, arrived at the zoo gates and mingled with members of the public gathered there. Grateful for their support, he shared his grief with them. Although he was shattered by the family's loss he wanted to say just a few simple words about his beloved son.

'Steve and I weren't like father and son—we were good mates,' he said. 'I'm a lucky guy. I've had the opportunity to have a son like Steve.'

He wanted the world to remember him as an 'ordinary bloke', which was why the family would be unlikely to accept the Queensland Government's offer of a state funeral. 'Steve would not have wanted that.'

Mr Irwin, the original owner of the zoo that Steve and his wife Terri later turned into a world-famous attraction, offered no excuses for the way his son died.

'He knew the risks he was taking. We had spoken about the risks in working among wildlife and yes, we knew we got through by experience and luck. Over the years, Steve and I have had a lot of adventures together, when anything could have gone wrong. Yes, he knew the risks involved with the type of work he was doing and he wouldn't have wanted it any other way.'

Mr Irwin had memories which would stay with him for the rest of his life. He spoke of their barbecues in the bush: 'Maybe we'd just wander off in the scrub and light a fire and maybe sit around the fire talking for hours on end, about nothing really.'

He had been about to bury a cow that had died calving when he heard that his son had been fatally stabbed by a stingray.

That previous month, Bob Irwin had been with Steve and his family in the Lakefield National Park. Steve, he said, had been in a good mood, 'probably the best I'd seen him for many years in his own attitude. He was peaceful and he was not under stress and he was doing something that he really loved doing and I won't ever forget that three or four weeks. I was very lucky.'

5

Born to the Wild

Since I was a boy I was out rescuing crocodiles and snakes.
My mum and dad were very passionate about that
and I was lucky enough to go along.

More than 4000 kilometres away from Batt Reef, Steve's wife of 14 years, Terri, along with their children Bindi Sue and young Bob, were enjoying the clean, fresh air near Cradle Mountain on the island of Tasmania, south of the Australian mainland. With its stunning waterland 'heart'—Dove Lake—it is little wonder that Cradle Mountain is part of the Tasmanian Wilderness World Heritage Area. For tourists, there are breathtaking bushwalking treks to be enjoyed, including the famous Overland Track, a six-day walking experience through some of the world's most beautiful mountain terrain.

Terri was there to enjoy a break with Bindi's teacher, Emma, who was celebrating her 30th birthday and to check on the welfare of the endangered Tasmanian devil. They'd already spent weeks with Steve in the bush at Cape York, in the far north of Australia but, as there was no room on Croc One for the family, Terri had headed off to Tasmania with Emma and the children.

Could there have been anything more intrusively shattering than to listen to a relative's voice over the phone telling her that Steve had been involved in a diving accident? On arrival at a motel, she had been asked to go straight into the manager's office and, in response to an urgent message, call her brother-in-law, Frank Muscillo, at the Australia Zoo.

Relaying that heart-stopping moment to interviewer Ray Martin on Australia's Channel Nine television network later she said Frank had told her: 'There's been a diving accident with Steve.'

She thought: 'Don't say it, don't say it, don't say it, don't say it.' Then she added: 'but he said it. He said those three words. He said: "And he died".'

'And I felt myself explode inside and I looked out the window and there is that beautiful little girl (Bindi) with her father's eyes looking at me with such joy because we were done with the research stuff and now we were going to just have fun. And I couldn't break down...'

The police were already on their way to pass on the news to Terri personally, but by then she was packing her bags and preparing to return home immediately by the time the official, shocking, message was relayed to her.

Friends were to reveal later that she put on a brave face for the sake of her children. She was being strong for herself, too. She made her way to Devonport airport for a chartered flight back to Queensland and a dash to the family home on the Sunshine Coast where friends and family members were waiting. She might have remembered Steve's words to her once if he lost control of a dangerous situation: 'Whatever you do, keep the cameras rolling.' She had responded: 'They aren't going to show it if you die.'

During the first few weeks following Steve's death, the world glimpsed Terri's personal agony through the words of her mother, Mrs Julie Raines, speaking to a American television network from her home in Oregon. Mrs Raines said her daughter was also concerned about the bleak future that lay ahead without Steve. Facing the months and years to come was a prospect she could not even contemplate, Terri had told her in a phone call. Her daughter was shattered.

'I'm struggling to cope right now,' she told her mother. 'I'm concerned about raising the children by myself.'

Mrs Raines, referring to the youngest child, added: 'Robert says "Where's Daddy?" She says Bindi's been a big help to her. Bindi's been a rock. It's just a very hard time.'

Her private grief was locked away behind the doors of the family home. There were tougher times to come. There was still the funeral and then perhaps a memorial service would follow. The public had shown they, too, wanted to farewell the man who had touched them in many ways. Terri mourned her soulmate away from the public gaze even though everyone wished her the best.

But a few days after Steve's death she sent a message to the zoo staff, thanking them for their support. Her first public statement was when she announced, through John Stainton, his memorial service would be held in the Crocoseum Steve had built and was proud of. At the same time she thanked the public for their 'overwhelming outpouring of love, support and prayers for her family.'

John Stainton said that their young daughter, Bindi, had already gained enough experience from her father to be able to fill his shoes and front up on television to host wildlife shows. Although only eight years old, she had already completed seven episodes of her own 26-part wildlife documentaries and it was, in fact, for Bindi's documentary that Steve had decided to swim with the stingrays.

'There will be a big void because Steve was such an iconic figure,' said John, himself struggling to come to terms with such a great loss. 'But I think his daughter will start to fill that void within the next 12 months to two years. I said to Steve a couple of months ago that she would eclipse him and he said he would love that.'

But then Steve had been all about 'family' and had been particularly proud of his 'little girl'. Even on that day before his tragic death he expressed his sadness that he could not be with Terri and the children because of his filming commitments. The family was seldom apart and they were often heard to remark that they played and worked together.

From Tasmania Bindi and Bob had sent a text message, through their mother. It said simply: 'The children send their love.'

How fitting it was that their life together had started in the zoo in 1991, when Terri was a 27-year-old naturalist on holiday from America. She had wanted to see in real life the larrikin Aussie she had heard so much about, this 'environmental Tarzan', the man who hand-fed the ferocious crocodiles at his parent's reptile park. First impressions for Terri were hardly appealing.

She watched as Steve Irwin scooped up a handful of chicken entrails, muscular legs bulging in the shortest of shorts. But then, moments before he was due to drop the food into the jaws of the waiting crocodile, he looked up—and his and Terri's eyes locked. He saw what he later described as 'the most beautiful girl I'd ever seen in my life'. For Terri it was 'love at first sight'.

After a whirlwind romance he went across to America and married Terri just eight months after they first met. But, he told Australian interviewer Andrew Denton on his program *Enough Rope* in 2004, he could not consummate the marriage on their wedding night because he was 'so scared, so anxious, so incredibly out of my element.'

As the television audience laughed, he went on: 'You know, we get back to, you know, a nice honeymoon suite and that and I, I, I was freaked.' But then he had a big steak and he was 'Okay'.

Returning to Australia for their honeymoon, Steve took his new bride away to a croc-infested river in Queensland where from time to time he would guide their small tin boat into the shallows for a 'quick, quiet tumble'. Years later Terri was to reveal that Steve was still 'hot' in the bedroom—and when he bent over for their croc-feeding shows at the zoo and she saw him still in those short shorts she would whistle loudly.

Their genuine and sincere love affair only served to enhance their popularity among the millions of their worldwide fans. They were likened to royalty, royalty of the jungles that is, a status that in one instance elevated them even above the King of Tonga.

King Taufa'ahau Tupou IV passed away in a New Zealand hospital a few days after Steve's tragic death and Prime Minister Helen Clark asked all councils to lower their flags to honour the ruler of the Pacific island kingdom. The town of Wanganui, on the North Island, refused. The Mayor, Michael Laws, said the king had ruled a 'corrupt country' and New Zealand should instead lower the flag for two Australians, Steve Irwin and well-known racing car driver Peter Brock, who had been killed in a car crash in the same tragic week as Steve's death.

'We did not lower the flag for them, so why on earth we would for this antediluvian king is beyond me,' said Laws. 'We honour people who have contributed to the community or the nation.'

The contribution that Steve was to make began when he was a young boy.

Seven years after Barry Humphries—through his alter-ego Dame Edna Everage—put the Melbourne suburb of Moonie Ponds on the world atlas, another star was born. Stephen Robert

Irwin came into the world on 22 February 1962, destined to become a child of the wild.

His destiny was decided from day one, for his parents, Bob, a plumber, and Lyn, were keen naturalists. His birth also coincided with his mother's birthday, so she and her husband saw his arrival as auspicious. A child is often only what his parents are, it is said, and truth of that could not be epitomised more than in the family background of the man who grew up to become the world's most popular eco-warrior.

Steve's father, Robert, was born at a time when the state of Victoria was reeling like the rest of the country from the Great Depression. After losing her husband in South East Asia during the Second World War, Steve's grandmother, Marjorie, struggled on alone to raise her son and his brother at their home in the Dandenong Ranges, a beautiful wooded region north east of Melbourne where the ringing call of the bellbird echoed through the forests.

So Bob Irwin, Steve's father, knew what it was like to be poor from an early age but he had an advantage over many of his young friends, for he was surrounded by the sounds of nature. He learned to identify the call of all the birds and knew where he could find a wombat, a snake or a possum at any time.

As Bob's family moved around Victoria in the earlier days, he met and fell in love with the woman who was to become his wife. Bob, who had started a trade as a plumber, married Lyn, who had embarked on a career as a maternity nurse, when he was 20 and she was two years younger. They moved into a house in the Melbourne suburb of Essendon, home of one of Victoria's big Australian rules football clubs, so it was not surprising that when their three children came along Steve and his two sisters, Joy and Mandy, embraced the enthusiasm of the game. It could hardly be avoided, for every Saturday the suburb was overflowing with fans wearing scarves and hats in their team's red and black colours.

Both Bob and Lyn Irwin were mad animal lovers and visitors to the Irwin home in Primrose Street had learned to tread carefully for they knew that in the back garden—and perhaps somewhere in the house—one reptile or more might be lurking. The young Steve quickly learned the art of handling them and his parents, proud of his skills and agreeing that he was ready and responsible, presented him with a birthday gift that made him the envy of all his friends at school—a 4-metre (12-foot) python.

The only stipulation was that Steve must never try to play with it, or even handle it, without his parents being around because the boy was about a third of its size and would have had no chance of freeing himself had the snake, which he christened Fred, decided to give him an overly friendly squeeze. Fred became the founder member of Steve's own small, private zoo, which was a kind of sub-branch of his parent's burgeoning menagerie.

Steve, despite his young age, was always able to show his parents that he was in control. At least on most occasions. There was one time, out in the bush in northern Victoria with his dad searching for more snakes along a river bank for their domestic zoo, that he came close to losing his life. With his father's attention distracted, Steve was confronted by a very large brown snake, its tongue flicking at Steve's plastic sandals—totally inadequate protection for a foray into the bush, he was to reflect later during his adult days when he would never dare to venture into the scrub without a good strong pair of boots.

The snake decided to back away and turned towards a rabbit burrow, but Steve wasn't going to let that 'little beauty' escape. He stamped his foot down on it, yelling to his father that he'd caught his first snake out in the wild. When Bob came racing through the shrubbery, he took one look at the scene of his son standing on a 2-metre (6-foot) brown snake and knocked the boy flying. Steve later learned how close he was to receiving a fatal bite from an Eastern Brown, the second most deadly snake on the planet. Aggressive when cornered, like most animals in the wild, they are the cause of more snakebite deaths in Australia than any other reptile.

In the family home as he was growing up—he recalled for television's *Enough Rope* host Andrew Denton—his mother would have 12 make-believe kangaroo pouches set up on the backs of chairs all around the house.

'So we'd have 12 little joeys, ranging from little pinkies all the way up to one-year-olds. You know, koalas hanging off the curtains, you know, with gum leaves stuck in there, sugar gliders gliding through. Like, you'd be walking down through the house … You're walking down through the house and next minute, clack, you know, on your bare back there'd be a possum—arggh!—rip into you. And of course, inside the house was just snakesville.'

'Really?' asked Denton.

'Oh, crikey, mate! Chock-a-block full of snakes.'

Steve's childhood friend and neighbour Tony Piscitelli recalled how Steve and his father would head off into the bush every weekend to look for additions to the amateur backyard zoo, while Lyn spent all her spare time caring for sick and injured wildlife.

'There were animals everywhere,' Tony remembered. 'Steve had an old pool out in the backyard. He had taken all the water out of it and filled it with sand and had reptiles living in there. We all thought he was a little crazy. He was, I suppose.'

But how did a boy who grew up thousands of kilometres from crocodile habitats learn how to fearlessly jump on their backs? While Steve was to learn those skills from his father in time, Tony Piscitelli provided a possible clue as to how some of that ability was acquired.

'We used to go to the local creek to do some fishing as kids and Steve wasn't scared to jump straight into the water and go for the carp in there. I reckon that's where it may have all started—him jumping straight down onto the carp, like he couldn't help himself.'

As their unofficial zoo grew to breaking point, the Irwin clan decided on a courageous step: they would move to Queensland's Sunshine Coast and run a wildlife sanctuary.

They were adept at caring for sick and injured animals and intuitively understood their habitats and needs. They were passionate, too, about conservation and the need to protect Australia's vanishing flora and fauna. They were convinced they could make a sanctuary work.

First they needed to find a suitable place. After scouring the region they purchased a four-acre block of land in 1970, but it was to be three tough years of clearing, digging and building before they were ready to open the doors. Little did the family realise the land they bought was to be the foundation of what is today the most famous private zoo in the world.

What was needed next were animals to fill the space—but not just any old creatures. The Irwins were already well known as amateur naturalists and had made a name for themselves as carers of maimed, orphaned or abandoned wildlife. So it was not long before their sanctuary became filled with the needy.

In 1973, when Steve was 11, the wildlife centre, then known as the Beerwah Reptile Park, opened up for the first time. What a contrast it was to today's slick Australia Zoo venture, but as Steve was to so often point out through his career, his parents had to start somewhere, learning all the way.

An early photograph shows his dad, Bob, dressed in a khaki shirt, very short shorts, white socks and a white bush hat, standing under the entrance sign. There are two large paintings of snakes, tongues flicking out, on each side of the mesh gates and a black-board offering the food available for visitors—cold drinks, sand-wiches, tea and coffee, ice creams, pies, sausage rolls and cakes. Early promotional brochures also featured an etching of a snake entwined around a tree branch. The Beerwah Reptile Park, on the Bruce Highway, offered 'all varieties of Australian reptiles' in a 'safe, natural habitat,' said the brochures. There was a list of what could be seen: death adders, black and brown snakes, pythons, tree snakes, goannas and lizards, etc. Almost all had been caught by Bob with the help of his young son and it was a 50 cents entry fee for adults to come in and view the animals and 15 cents for children.

Steve idolised his parents, copying his father in everything that he did, while he saw his mother as a kind of saint on earth when it came to rehabilitating wildlife in trouble. 'Mother Nature? My mum was Mother Nature,' he once said of her.

If his mum was Mother Nature, he saw his father as Father Nature. It was he who had pioneered humane and distinctly unique techniques for catching venomous snakes and crocodiles that needed to be moved from one place to another and in time he won the support of the Queensland National Parks and Wildlife Service as an official 'croc catcher'.

He began taking young Steve with him on his crocodile hunting expeditions—in fact there was no way Steve was going to be left behind—instructing him how to capture crocodiles. While using a trap was the safest, sometimes a trap wasn't always readily available and the next best thing, and certainly the quickest, was the personal approach—jumping on a crocodile's back and restraining it with an arm around its jaws. For the uninitiated it seemed like tempting fate, but young Steve put his entire trust in his father's wisdom and teachings, whether it was handling crocodiles or deadly snakes without being bitten.

Back at the Beerwah Reptile Park, Lyn continued to administer to her orphaned young charges—kangaroos and their joeys—and other creatures that landed there. There was still much to learn. There was a big difference between having a hobby collection of reptiles in a Melbourne back garden and operating a private zoo that was rapidly filling with every kind of Australian animal imaginable.

Lyn looked to the animals themselves to teach her how to care for them. She was extremely sensitive to their needs, studying their behaviour and watching how her particular nursing techniques were either rejected or accepted. If any animal showed signs of distress she would change tack and try to comfort it in another way. Steve had often spoken of his mother as a pioneer in wildlife rehabilitation, for in the late sixties and early seventies little was known about raising the orphaned creatures of the Australian bush. Her joey pouches, similar to those that had been hung around the house in Melbourne, were still the most successful way of making a young kangaroo comfortable, and keeping it close to its natural life in a mother's pouch.

While she had her hands full with animals, Lyn was also careful to keep a watchful eye over her son. She once described him as 'on the verge of being hyperactive; if he went missing, you would always look up a tree and there he'd be.'

Steve was a gap-toothed, nine-year-old, sandy-haired schoolboy with a kind of Beatle haircut when he caught his first crocodile. A colony of freshwater crocs were about to lose their waterhole in the Gulf of Carpentaria because it was going to be emptied, and they required relocation. The job fell to Bob Irwin.

'Come on,' Bob said to Steve, 'let's do this together.'

There was an eeriness about the scene as Steve and his father manoeuvred a small tin boat through the still water at night, using a powerful spotlight to pick out what appeared to be the glowing eyes of the crocodiles. Freshwater crocodiles—'freshies'—are considered to be far safer than their saltwater cousins which tend to lurk around river estuaries, but there could be no assumptions. Every animal had to be treated with the utmost respect. The smallest mistake could be fatal.

Steve watched as his father would dive off the boat, grab a crocodile around the neck then toss it into the small craft where Steve would jump on it and hold it until Bob was able to secure its mouth and legs. Soon afterwards, the enthusiastic boy was leaping into the waterhole to catch his first ever crocodile. It put up a fight as it rolled with Steve on its back in a desperate attempt to shake him off. The youngster refused to let go and finally his father hauled him and the croc aboard.

Steve Irwin had been 'blooded'. Within a year he knew exactly what he had to do without directions from his father.

It was the tropical jungles of northern Australia, in the far north of Queensland, teaming with waterways, colourful butterflies, snakes and of course crocodiles that had fascinated him as a boy when he travelled there on field trips with his father and sometimes both his parents. He learned the hard way about the tricks and traps of the rainforest, including a prolific and dangerously prickly vine known to locals as the 'wait a while'. Its name comes from the way it hooks into the skin or clothes and only releases its victim if he very slowly unhitches the barbs. Locals also knew it as the 'lawyer vine'—explaining that once it got hold of you it wouldn't let you go until you had half-bled to death. Fortunately, when Steve blundered into a thick patch of the plant, was caught and held, his mother was on hand to untangle him. Another few deep scratches to add to his growing collection of scars.

The bush, though, held him enthralled. He decided that he would be a zoologist, although he was already halfway to believing that had been his destiny from earlier days. What he was determined to do was get out of school as soon as possible, but he had to wait until he was 17 before he could leave Caloundra State High School. He hadn't enjoyed it much, explaining later that he didn't have time for books.

What he did enjoy reading was surf magazines and when he wasn't out with his father in the bush somewhere he was to be found riding the waves off Caloundra, a popular seaside resort, or spear fishing. An old family photograph shows him as a teenager, with a mop of long blond hair, proudly posing with a spear gun in one hand and a large fish in the other. In fact, Steve proved himself to be more than capable on the sports ground or in the water, whether it was cricket, football, swimming or surfing.

The teenager had matured and was ready to take on just about anything whenever or wherever a challenge presented itself. One instance he recalled was a game of cricket in his school days. Having been bowled out, he wandered off to search a nearby waterway for lizards. He found instead an attractive gecko, but as he went to pounce on it he found himself staring into the hissing face of a venomous red-bellied black snake. He had learned from his father to 'read' a snake in a strike position and this one was seconds away from attacking him. Carefully, the boy backed off and he thanked his lucky stars that the reptile had not struck because its speed would have given him no chance.

The confrontation between boy and snake was not over yet. He was determined to prove himself to his father by bagging a snake to add to the reptile family at the wildlife park. So he moved in on the creature. The red-bellied black struck out at him, narrowly missing him. A second strike of those deadly fangs glanced off his boot. Then, as the snake slid away, Steve grabbed it by the tail but made sure he kept its body on the grass as his father had shown him, so that it could concentrate on trying to get away rather than strike at him again.

Calling to a school friend nearby, he asked him to bring a sack or something to drop the snake into. The friend returned with the school bus driver's 'eskie'—cooler box—and Steve, watched by his anxious friend, carefully lowered the snake in. It was not over yet. The young Irwin realised that this was a good area for red-bellied blacks and proceeded to hunt for more as his school cricket team played on. As his own turn to bat had passed with a miserable duck, he had all the time in the world. Several more venomous reptiles were added to that day's tally. It was a very edgy bus driver who, having learned the contents of the cooler box, sped the boys back to their destination. His father was far from pleased. Once again, Steve had taken too many risks with some of the most dangerous creatures in the wild.

Steve had certainly earned his stripes as a proficient crocodile catcher, thanks to his father's careful and watchful training procedures. To add to Bob Irwin's dismay, Steve continued to venture into scrubby bushes and desert rocks to capture reptiles, spiders and lizards.

It was becoming clear he had specific empathy with dangerous creatures, especially those that were disdained by his peers.

'Funny thing, I wasn't too scared of dying from black snake envenomation, but I was shaking in my boots at the thought of losing dad's pride in me, the bloke I respect and admire the most, the bloke responsible for the person I am today,' he wrote in his 1997 book *The Crocodile Hunter*, co-authored by his wife Terri. For, he said in later years, 'I wanted to be my dad more than anything. And now I am, and then some.'

Steve Irwin was the child who was destined to never really grow up, many of his friends were to say of him. Perhaps, they agreed, it was the influence of the incredible adventures he had as a young-ster—adventures he never wanted to leave behind as the years took him into adulthood. He loved to give funny names to some of the animals and birds living at the reptile park, including Curley, a curlew who thought she was an emu; Egg Head, who thought he was a human and a brolga called Brolly.

During his teenage years, he knocked about with a group of friends who drove battered old Ford Falcons and Valiants along the coastal roads, whistling at girls, playing football and grabbing every chance to catch a wave. The young Irwin played as a second rower for the Caloundra Sharks while at sea he found good waves between Kings Beach and Wurtulla. He was not afraid of the water, no matter how big the waves were. Nor did he fear what swam below.

His friend of 30 years, Chris White, told Brisbane's *Sunday Mail* that there was no high school out at Landsborough, in the hinterland, so Steve and other teenagers from the country had to catch the bus each day to Caloundra High. That was where he and his brother Mick met Steve and it wasn't long before their friend became a kind of surrogate brother—Chris's parents' third child. Because Steve lived some 19 kilometres (11 miles) from the beach he would often spend three days a week at the White home in Caloundra and at weekends Steve, Mick, Chris and another surfer, Jeff Allchin, would meet at dawn and cruise the coast in a rusty old white Mazda.

'At that point, Steve was still learning, but he was a tenacious surfer and although he didn't have a lot of technical skills he was strong and powerful and determined,' said Chris. But it was that determination that would see him get hurt often. One day Chris knew Steve had injured himself because he saw him coming up over the embankment holding his arm and without his board.

'He'd received a fin chop that sliced his bicep open. We ran to the shop where Steve placed his arm on the drinks cabinet and his whole muscle fell out. He just fiddled around and put it back in. The pain was not a worry—even though he got 52 stitches.'

What had not been known generally until Chris revealed it was that while Steve continued to help his parents at the zoo, when he left school he also became an apprentice diesel fitter for Maroochy Council. Despite that injury to his arm, he became part of the established 25-strong clan of sunburned Caloundra wave riders. They were a group who loved the outdoors, recalled old friend Ross Ginns, who still lives in Caloundra. Many of them went on to be rangers, pilots and firemen. When Steve finished his apprenticeship he went into full-time work with his father.

'Even while we were at school, Steve was always going off chasing crocodiles with his dad up north,' Ross, now 44, told the Sunday Mail. 'Over the years many of the group lost touch, but still met at a local tavern each Christmas Eve.'

There was a steady stream of visitors to the reptile park so that by 1980, with its facilities upgraded, it was renamed the Queensland Reptile and Fauna Park. The public continued to bring in orphaned creatures to be cared for by Lyn. Her skills were now quite famous in the area while Steve and his dad went on with their crocodile conservation work.

He was getting to understand and love the ancient reptiles more and more. Little did he know that one day he would be internationally famous as 'the Crocodile Hunter'.

Inevitably, the time came when Steve and his father decided to upgrade—and try to help saltwater crocodiles that needed relocating. Some were known as 'rogue crocs', reptiles that posed a threat to humans. Steve and his dad worked with the Queensland National Parks and Wildlife Service in relocating them under what was known as a crocodile management program.

One day word reached them that a particular reptile, a large, dark-skinned crocodile with a very unfriendly nature, was causing concern to fishermen and cane farmers in the north of Queensland.

The Irwins searched rivers over a period of 18 months, laying baits and traps to no avail. Then, when he was alone, Steve had the surprise of his life—the monster crocodile was in a trap he'd laid. Steve realised that there was no way he could handle the reptile on his own, so he drove to a nearby homestead and collected a group of men.

With the added assistance of a front end loader, the crocodile, now tethered, was lifted onto dry land. Rangers later arrived and winched the huge creature, blindfolded with a sack to ease his stress, into a crate. The croc was sent by rail to the Irwin reptile park where, as Steve was to record later, his father ensured the reptile was 'treated like royalty'. The reptile's life had been saved, for Steve believed that in time someone would have shot him because of the threat he posed.

6

Love at First Sight

My number one rule is to keep that camera rolling.
Even if it's shaky or slightly out of focus, I don't give a rip!

When I met Steve in 1998 he led me around the path at the zoo to an enclosure containing a huge crocodile called Agro. 'Now this little number,' he said with a huge grin, 'could give you a very nasty bite if you don't get out of the way quickly enough.'

Then he relayed the story of how he'd caught it, again to save its life because it was a dead certainty, he had believed, that someone would shoot it because it was posing a threat to cane farmers' children. He didn't like the idea of any reptile being killed and he was now convinced that he had a very serious role to play in relocating those animals that people feared and believed threatened their safety.

Steve was to recall an incident in the mid–1980s when a middle-aged woman decided to go swimming at night in territory that was alive with crocodiles. She was grabbed by a 3.5-metre (11-foot) crocodile and eaten—and the result was that more than 200 reptiles were killed in the following weeks by local people venting their anger on any crocodile they could find.

When he found Agro, he was on his own, apart from his dog, Chilli. But he still decided to have a go at capturing it anyway. It seemed like sheer madness, but by now Steve Irwin had a great confidence in his own abilities. Agro was caught in a trap, a long steel mesh enclosure, after it had gone in to take some bait. While Steve worked at securing the trap to his small boat the croc lashed out with its head, butting the side of the boat with a great deal of force.

Steve grabbed its tail and began hauling the creature aboard, much to the terror of Chilli the dog. Such was the struggle that Steve decided he was safer in the water than in the boat. He grabbed his dog under his arm and jumped in up to his armpits. The crocodile smashed its head into the side of the boat, making a huge dent. It was still mainly in the cage, so Steve threw a rope over both the crocodile and the boat, then dived under several times to tie the creature to the side of the boat. Then, with the crocodile secured, he fired up the outboard motor and headed back to his bush camp. There, he managed to drag a wooden crate close to it and, with a little help from Chilli, who bit the croc on the tail, he was able to get it into the crate.

Steve related to me how Agro was always trying to get even with him for catching him. The croc had smashed a couple of lawnmowers, a shovel and had eaten one of Steve's hats. 'I understand his territorialism and try hard not to upset him,' Steve wrote later, 'but if he sees, hears, or smells me he'll submerge and poise for an ambush.' What was it that attracted Steve to crocodiles? 'It's just something that was born into me, mate,' he said as we chatted near Agro's pen. 'But then there was my parents' upbringing. There were animals all around me from the day I was born. I was always going to be a child of the wild and then a wild man!'

Everywhere he went in his early days as a Crocodile Hunter, Steve preached the croc gospel. He wanted people to understand that although they are a dangerous animal, they did not deserve to be indiscriminately killed just because humans were naturally afraid of them. His message is simple: Australia, not having hunting mammals like lions or bears, was the land of the reptile and crocodiles that dated back to prehistoric times. What we saw today was close to how they looked nearly 70 million years ago. Their territory in ancient times ranged right up into Thailand and on to the Bay of Bengal, but in modern times their wholesale slaughter had pushed them to the brink of extinction. Only in northern Australia can their numbers be considered stable, he said. In Asia, in particular they were quickly dying out.

He listened with interest as I told him of a story I had written some years before of a giant crocodile known in the Malay language as 'the easy-going bachelor'. It had earned the name because it did not have a mate and swam lazily up and down a river in Borneo, south of Kuching.

Measuring about 5 metres (16 feet) long, it was being blamed for the death of at least 10 villagers in as many years. The police had tried to shoot it. The army had tried to blow it up by throwing hand grenades at it. Fishermen had tried to trap it in their nets. All to no avail. The toll among the crocodile population was high as many 'innocent' creatures were killed in the all-out attempts to eliminate the rogue reptile.

Then a large crocodile, suspected of being the easy-going bachelor, was shot dead with a barrage of police bullets and hauled ashore. Its stomach was cut open to establish whether it had any human remains—and the villagers who crowded around reeled back when they saw, in its stomach, the almost complete body of a child, a young boy, with only a slight wound to a hand.

Just about that time reports were being received of a child who had gone missing several hours earlier while bathing in the river. Someone had shouted 'crocodile' as he and others were washing themselves and the boy, his eyes blinded by soap, dived the wrong way—straight into the jaws of the crocodile, which had swallowed him virtually whole. But the monster was not the easy-going bachelor, for that large croc was caught much later, and it was only by chance that the killer of the boy had been caught.

Steve's eyes widened with amazement. 'Crikey!' he said. 'That is one heck of a croc story. But do you believe it?'

'Oh, I believe it all right. I went to a crocodile farm run by a Malay known as Crocodile Johnson and he had a photograph of the child lying beside the dead croc on a sheet of tarpaulin, with villagers crowded around staring down at the boy, whose skin had turned white and he looked like a ghost child.'

'Crikey!' Steve said again.

There was only one love in Steve's life as he went into manhood—and that was the bush and the creatures that roamed in it. Working with his parents in the zoo was a full-time job but fate was soon to bring about a major change in his life and turn Steve Irwin from an unknown naturalist into an international star.

Fate for Steve had a name—and her name was Terri Raines, of Eugene, Oregon. On what was her second visit to Australia, in the summer months of 1991, Terri travelled with a girlfriend, leaving behind a wildlife rehabilitation centre and a part-time job in an emergency veterinary hospital. She, too, had no time for a social life, but when her friend asked her to travel to Australia with her she thought 'the heck with the cost, I'm going!'

Terri's father was running a successful building business and it was he who had first inspired her loving care for animals when he brought home injured creatures he'd found while driving around the highways. By the mid-1980s, Terri was in charge of her own business, a rehabilitation centre called Cougar Country where injured raccoons, bears, bobcats, possums and foxes were treated and prepared for their release back into territory where they were thought to have been roaming.

Soon Terri and her staff found themselves caring for up to 300 animals a year. She wanted to broaden her skills, so she joined the emergency veterinary hospital in 1989. Her life was full—helping her father run the family business, rehabilitating animals, putting in hours at the vet hospital and tending for a personal animal family of her own—no less than 15 cats, a number of birds and a dog. Romance … it was not a word she was well acquainted with given the time and energy required to care for her many charges. At least not until she arrived in Australia.

During their travels along the east coast, Terri and her girl-friend stopped at the Queensland Reptile and Fauna Park. It was, after all, a taste of home, even though the animals would be entirely different. Hurry, she and her friend were told, or they would miss the crocodile-feeding demonstration.

She was just in time to see Steve beginning his popular after-noon 'show'. Terri watched mesmerised as he calmly fed meat to a huge crocodile 'looking more like he was mailing a letter than depositing food into bone-crushing jaws,' she was to recall. She could not help noticing how he spoke with genuine love and affection about a crocodile that could have so easily consumed the keeper himself.

She hurried around to another pen where 'the keeper' was due to start another crocodile feeding demonstration. This was to be the moment when true love struck. Captivated by his enthusiasm for crocodiles, she found her focus shifting from the animals to the man who was speaking with such passion about them. He told briefly of his adventures in the bush, trapping crocodiles at night from a small boat.

Terri was to recall asking: 'Who was this man who spoke so casually of jumping into the water to wrestle crocodiles? He looked about my age and wasn't wearing a wedding ring, but surely this wonderful guy must have already been snapped up by some lucky girl. How could I possibly get a chance to talk to him, anyway?'

She need not have worried. As she edged her way out of the crowd after the demonstration 'his eyes met mine'. It was, she recalled, as if we had always known each other. He introduced himself and they became lost in conversation, the minutes turning into an hour, which Terri prayed would go on and on. She was to confess later that she had trouble understanding his Australian accent. She had to keep interrupting his enthusiastic rapid-fire speech with 'excuse me?' and 'I'm sorry, what was what?' By the time she had to leave, she still had not learned whether this man she had been so smitten by had a girlfriend, a fiancee or a wife. He grinned at her and, as if he'd read her thoughts, asked if she'd like to meet his girlfriend.

Her heart sank, but she tried not to show it. She didn't care to meet the woman in Steve's life, even as he called Sui to come to him. To Terri's surprise and delight, Sui turned out to be a small Staffordshire dog which, Steve said with a big grin spreading across his face at Terri's obvious relief, he loved dearly. He gave her a brochure with his name and phone number written on it, said he hoped they could meet up again.

What she hadn't realised was that they were both feeling the same emotions for each other. 'When I saw her first, our eyes seemed to meet and for a moment I forgot all about the crocodile that would have probably killed me if I continued to look at her,' he recalled.

Terri had another way of putting it. 'I think I fell in love with him at first sight because he's the first guy I met that I couldn't chase with a snake. He wasn't scared. It was very attractive … there's this guy in this zoo doing a crocodile demonstration, talking about crocs the way I'd never heard before and, you know like they're, they're really passionate lovers, wonderful mothers, and he desperately loved crocodiles. And I thought "What is it with this guy?" … Here was this like "reptile man meets mammal woman" and it was fantastic. We just fell desperately in love.'

As for Steve, he was to tell television host Andrew Denton: 'Mate, it was love at first sight you know when we met at the zoo … I hadn't seen any sheila for a couple of years—I'd been up catching crocs. And she did this real wiggly cougar thing and stuff.' Whatever he meant by that was left to the imagination for a moment, before Terri explained.

'I was just telling him about cougars because he'd say to me you know here's how crocodiles launch a strike from the water's edge. So I said it's really funny cause when you're with a cougar what you've got to watch out for is when you see this.' Then she stood and wiggled, before continuing: 'As soon as you see this you know they're about to pounce.'

'So mate,' said Steve, continuing the story of their meeting, 'she's turned up from the beach, I've been out in the scrub for like two years catching crocs, she turns up and does this and I'm standing there going "woohoo!"'

'Your first love was a cougar called Melina,' said Denton. 'Your second love was Steve—is there a pattern here at all?'

'From one beast to another,' she quickly replied. 'It's true—Beauty and the Beast.'

Back in Brisbane after that first meeting, Terri could not contain her feelings. She rang Steve and asked if she could come back to the wildlife park again while her friend Lori spent the day scuba diving. Not only did he enthusiastically invite her back, he said she could stay for the entire weekend. She was introduced to his sister Mandy, his mother and his father. Terri told Steve and his family about her own work in America rescuing cougars. She stayed at a nearby motel that weekend, seizing every chance to listen to the stories of Steve's forays into the bush to capture crocodiles and snakes and relocate them or bring them back to the park if they were in need of medical attention.

On their first date, dinner at the nearby resort town of Caloundra, they sat down for a seafood buffet. She saw what she thought was a misty look in his eyes and braced herself for him to say something romantic, only to hear something quite different. Staring at the crabmeat and juice that had spilled down her arms he commented: 'Gosh, you're not ladylike at all!'

She was at least expecting a first kiss when he dropped her back at the hotel, but it was not to be—he simply said it had been a very fine evening and he'd be back first thing in the morning. As promised, he was there, but the day was no romantic trip around the district. Instead, Terri found herself sweating under a blazing Queensland sun, rake in hand as she set about cleaning up the leaves in the park. But then, the trip came. Steve drove Terri around to the local sights but again failed to seize the chance to give her a kiss as they stood at a lookout and gazed at the distant mountains. The following day he drove her to Brisbane where she boarded the flight to America, convinced on one hand that he had lost interest in her, but feeling also that fate was drawing them together.

A few weeks later her phone rang. She recognised that Aussie drawl immediately. There was small talk about crocodiles and cougars and then came a stunning announcement: he was coming over to visit her.

The ten days they spent together in America were 'magical' she recalled and it was painful for her to say goodbye to him once again. They agreed to meet again and next time it would be her turn to visit him. It was just two months later after many phone calls that Terri touched down at Brisbane airport, her heart pounding with expectation at what the future might hold. In fact, it was mostly work—and getting to meet a small crocodile which Steve insisted she hold. It was so tiny, in fact, that when it tried to bite her finger she hardly felt a thing. With some of the mundane chores and house-keeping out of the way after the first few days of Terri's visit, they boarded his truck and he drove her to the north of Queensland where he was interested in surveying the crocodiles in a particular river system.

She was enchanted by the tropical scenery … fast flowing rivers tumbling over boulders against a backdrop of thick rainforest. When darkness fell in Steve's book it was no time to call it a day—it was time to start work, for this was the best time to spot crocodiles, aiming a torch across the river to pick out those glowing red balls that were the reflections of the light in their eyes. Although Terri, sitting in their small boat, could hear things splashing near the boat, Steve assured her that they weren't anywhere near crocodiles yet—what she was hearing were tortoises fish and frogs going about their nocturnal business, and that sudden fluttering above was nothing more than fruit bats.

They were incredible days out there in the bush, the excitement enhanced by an apparent attack on Sui the dog by a herd of wild pigs, and although Steve and Terri were concerned that she might have sustained serious internal injuries, she recovered after a couple of days. They looked at crocodile nests with eggs still in them and tramped through the undergrowth, laughing as they went and Terri found herself falling for Steve in a big way. I'm definitely in love, she admitted to herself. Later, she recalled one night in particular: 'I was nearly asleep when I heard Steve's voice out of the darkness quietly asking me if it was still tradition to ask a girl's father first before proposing. I'm not sure what I said. My heart was pounding so hard I was sure Steve could hear it. I lay away long into the night. I had a lot to think about.'

Nothing more was said about marriage when they returned to the reptile park at Beerwah but she could feel the excitement, the electricity, between them. One evening as they sat under a spreading fig tree in the park grounds, right in the middle of a conversation about wildlife—what else?—Steve dropped the question. Would she marry him?

'It wasn't as if I hadn't thought about this moment,' she wrote in their co-authored book. 'I just never expected it so soon. Four months earlier Steve and I didn't even know each other. Then I heard a little voice say "Yes, I will." The little voice was mine. It must have been! In the midst of this emotional moment, Steve's mum came out looking for us. She knew immediately what was going on and ran off to tell Steve's dad. The next few days were a rush of celebration—telling the staff, parties, calling my parents, and trying to figure out a wedding date. We decided to marry in June. The wedding would be in my hometown in Oregon. Steve invited me to stay in Australia until the wedding, but I knew I had to get back. I would have less than four months to get ready to change my life for ever.'

So the staff at the zoo became part of Terri's life, just as she became part of theirs. Her forthcoming marriage to Steve would, indirectly, be her marriage to them. It explained years later when Steve was to die so tragically, why her loss was their loss, and their loss was hers.

On her return to America after accepting Steve's hand in marriage, Terri set about arranging the wedding and, with a pain in her heart, looking for someone who would be suitable to take over her animal rehabilitation centre, Cougar Country. While she was able to find a temporary helper, she sadly accepted that the business would have to close after that if she were to help Steve with his own wildlife work in Australia. Fortunately, she was able to find homes for all the animals—at least those which could not be released to the wild because, hand reared they would not have been able to adapt.

It was while Terri was in America that Steve, for the first time, came close to losing his life. He wanted to move one of the bigger crocs, Graham, from his enclosure and away from other crocodiles there because he was growing too big and also becoming aggressive towards the others.

Graham, 3.7 metres (12 feet) long and weighing 350 kilograms (771 pounds), had been caught by Steve near Townsville in northern Queensland in 1988 after frightening the locals by loitering around a boat ramp. Steve believed that Graham had a long memory and never forgave him for catching him.

Steve, already the young showman, invited Channel Ten to film his attempt to get Graham from the pen by offering him a piece of meat. His plan then was to toss a loop over Graham's mouth, drag the animal from the water, blindfold him and secure him. But it did not go accordingly. Almost as if Graham suspected a trick, he refused to emerge from the water. Steve tried again several days later, again with the television cameraman standing by.

The third time around Graham slowly waddled out of the water as Steve dangled the bait from his hand, ready with the lasso in the other. Suddenly Graham leaped and in a flash had hold of Steve's right hand. To the horror of staff and the camera crew—who kept filming—Graham began to drag Steve towards the water and, fearing he would cause serious damage to himself if he tried to struggle, Steve allowed the croc to pull him along. In the water, with his arm still in the croc's jaws, Steve fell on top of the reptile, resulting in the croc releasing the arm. Bleeding badly from the bites that had gone right through his hand, Steve was rushed to hospital, but not before he checked that Channel Ten had captured the incident on camera.

Terri was to recall later that when she spoke to Steve from America that night as they looked forward to their wedding, he admitted he had made a mistake. 'This wasn't an easy situation for me to handle,' she wrote in her shared book. 'It was a mistake that could have cost Steve his life.'

While it might be considered unfair to raise the topic after his death, it is a question that must be asked. What if the same 'mistake' had occurred when, years later, he had tempted a large crocodile with bait while holding baby Bob in his arms? The incident caused outrage around the world and raised serious questions about his common sense and whether his success had gone to his head. Steve insisted in the wake of the row that Bob was very safe and there was no chance at all of an accident occurring—and in any case, he said, the camera angle had given the impression that the crocodile was much closer to him and the baby than was suggested.

His wounds healed and, after two weeks, Steve was finally able to capture Graham and move him to a new pond. Steve was then ready to fly to America with his family and friends and then the wedding was upon them. Hundreds of family and friends were there to watch the two wildlife lovers take their vows before posing for their formal wedding photographs, Steve unrecognisable in his dark wedding suit and bow tie, his scarred hand hidden behind the bouquet that Terri, in a flowing white gown and a floral tiara, held.

'I've been busted up, had cartilage operations, had my chest ripped to bits—blood and broken bones are no big deal,' he said later. 'But the pain of standing there in a suit with a tie around my neck, I tell ya, I'd sooner have a python around me neck.'

If Terri had dreamed of a sunbaked honeymoon at some exotic resort, she had much to learn about her boy from the bush. They travelled around Oregon for a few days before Steve heard that a large crocodile needed to be relocated in Queensland. They looked at one another for a moment—before agreeing that they should continue their honeymoon as 'Crocodile Hunters'.

So they headed back to Australia to continue the 'honeymoon'—not on a luxury cruiser like other newlyweds but in a tin boat in the north of the state looking for a huge reptile that could chomp either one of them up for dinner. Terri had happily gone along with the idea of wading through remote and dangerous river systems, for the adventure was to be captured on film—their first joint documentary. Little did they realise that those first action shots were to be the start of a major international project which was, over the years, to inspire generations around the world.

Accompanying the khaki-clad couple on their mosquito-plagued honeymoon was a film crew who followed their four-wheel drive with the tin boat on the roof, into the depths of the tropics. It was not long before Terri learned just how dangerous the bush could be. Looking for a toilet spot she almost stood on a large, poisonous red-bellied black snake. Her screams brought Steve running. He grabbed the reptile by the tail and carried it far away from their camp.

The larger crocodile that was the purpose of their working honeymoon had been worrying people who lived on the edge of the river system. Steve, whose reputation as a Crocodile Hunter had spread rapidly with each successful croc relocation in Australia's tropical north, had been asked to move this reptile to another area—if he could even find it. When they did, Terri learned something more about the bush: that sometimes the locals decide to take matters into their own hands.

The crocodile was no longer a threat—someone with a gun had tracked it down and killed it. If there was a croc killer around, it meant that others were likely to be targeted too. So the new Mr and Mrs Irwin set out to look for the shot crocodile's female mate—a tiring task that involved dragging the tin boat across stretches of dry land.

During the night they were plagued by mosquitoes and creatures that Terri could not identify made all kinds of curious sounds. Exhaustion, though, takes its toll on even the hardiest of bush people and Terri was soon fast asleep. As the days and nights passed, she became more accustomed to the noises and the dangers, although Steve impressed upon her she should always keep her eyes open for anything and never assume there was nothing around to bite her.

Eventually they found the female crocodile's nest and Steve showed Terri how to set up a trap. Like the previous traps he had laid, it consisted of a long rectangular cage of thick mesh. When a crocodile enters to take a bait, the door drops and the crocodile is caught. Several days passed before there were any developments. In the meantime the couple and the film crew explored the bush, playing out scenes that were to be repeated hundreds of times in years to come. They filmed a large goanna foraging in the river bank sand for food and later, to even Steve's amazement, they found the goanna's nest containing 12 eggs—which were hatching. They were never to witness such a phenomenon again.

As they continued to explore they came across two farmers who told the group of their concerns about a large crocodile that was living in a dam near one of their homes. The men were concerned about their families, while Steve was worried, on hearing that the dam level was dropping, that the crocodile would die when the water ran out.

After examining the dam, Steve announced that no trap was necessary. He had estimated from the marks in the mud that the crocodile was 'no longer' than 2.5 metres (8 feet) long and he could capture it by jumping on its back, restraining it, blindfolding it and carting it off to a new location where there was plenty of water. He would need the assistance of one of the crew, Wes Mannion, who was, in fact, the wildlife park's manager and, of course, Terri's help would be needed, too. Wes and Terri did not relish the idea of going out onto the water at night in a tin boat to catch a crocodile but agreed to rely on Steve's knowledge and expertise.

Their torchlight soon picked out the crocodile's red eyes—one sure way of finding a reptile at night.

I had personally experienced this when I stayed for a few days in the heart of the Kakadu National Park—where the *Crocodile Dundee* movies were partially shot—with one of the caretakers of the disused Ranger uranium mine near the tiny community of Jabiru. The mine was territory that could only be entered with permission so I was privileged to be able to stay in the caretaker's house. After dinner he took me out onto the verandah and said: 'If you can't sleep, do not, under any circumstances go for a wander down there during the night'—and he pointed to where a large dark stretch of water lay.

'Oh, you think I might fall in or something?' I asked, naively.

'No,' he said, switching on his torch and directing the beam towards the water. 'Because of them.' The beam picked up what seemed like scores of tiny red lights. 'They're croc eyes. They're all down there waiting for you.'

Needless to say, I remained secure in my bed for the entire night.

Steve Irwin waded into the water, dragging a net along with him. It would have seemed like madness to both his wife and the film crew but even as he struggled to get the net around the reptile they had found he kept up a running commentary for the camera.

Finally he managed it and moments later Terri found herself grabbing the creature by its tail and helping to haul it onto the embankment. After further struggles, they succeeded in getting it into a long container, ready to be taken to a new home in the river.

As time went by on that first trip—and the team waited to catch the crocodiles—Terri learned just how experienced her hero husband was. Later in their jointly written book she explained something of his technique: 'Jumping a crocodile is not simply a matter of flinging oneself off the bow of the boat and grabbing it. A good jump takes precision and timing. When Steve jumps a croc, he must aim right for the neck. His hands will push the crocodile's face away from his own to avoid a nasty bite. Steve's legs wrap around the crocodile's tail to keep it from swimming off with him.

'Here is the catch: if Steve were to aim for the crocodile's neck and the croc saw him coming, the crocodile would submerge. In order for the croc to submerge, it slips backward in the water first. Once it's under the water, the crocodile tucks its legs to its sides and uses that huge, powerful tail to propel it through the water nearly as fast as a dolphin! Therefore Steve tries to aim for the crocodile's mid-section—as the croc retreats, Steve lands precisely on its neck. This works really well unless the crocodile stays where it is. In which case, Steve could end up grabbing the croc mid-body, and the shocked crocodile could easily swing around and give Steve a nasty bite!'

What many of Terri's friends have found astonishing is just how quickly she learned about crocodile catching—and how very courageous she was in those early hunting days with her husband. The thought of an inexperienced young woman leaping into swamp water with a crocodile and trying to haul it away from its watery environment sent shivers up the spines of those who listened to Terri's early exploits.

On this honeymoon trip, as they waited for the big crocodile to swim into the trap, Steve tried to catch a smaller creature. But he found himself in trouble when the crocodile decided it wasn't going to co-operate. While he gripped its body, the crocodile dragged him under several times and Terri, watching from the tin boat, realised he needed help. What should she do? What any superwoman would do—she jumped straight in, grabbed the crocodile by the tail and, with her feet slipping on the muddy bottom, began to help Steve drag it towards the bank. What they needed was a blindfold to lessen its fear, so Terri ripped off Steve's shirt and they made do with that. The makeshift blindfold calmed the crocodile and they were finally able to bring it to the shore in preparation for relocation.

At last the large reptile they were looking for entered the trap and the gate dropped down. They had her, an old lady aged around 40 years. Terri felt unhappy about moving her, but it was either that or leave her to be killed by a hunter with a gun. Because the trap was now higher up from the water surface, as the estuary tide had dropped, he had to virtually take a ride on the back of the tethered crocodile down over the bank and into the boat, an astonishing scene all captured on camera.

As a first-ever episode for the couple's wildlife series, they were collecting some eye-popping footage. The big crocodile was eventually released in another remote part of the river where she did not pose a threat to any nearby properties and where it was hoped she would be safe from a poacher's gun.

Terri had shown herself to be a very quick learner. She shared Steve's passion and agreed with him that if we had a world without crocodiles it would be like having rivers without souls. Each day Steve taught her more. He described to Terri all the tiny signs that a creature, not just a crocodile, will exhibit before it readies itself to make a strike and take a bite. Above all, he made the point over and over that one could never relax when in close proximity to any wild animal. The senses had to be primed at all times, eyes ever watchful.

That first film sequence, put out under the title *The Crocodile Hunter,* was an immediate hit, due to Steve's dazzling presentation and death-defying antics and—apart from her own courage—Terri's foresight. For that first film was to pave the way for the international spread of Steve Irwin's own kind of gospel; the gospel of the bush. With the involvement of the man who was to become his manager, John Stainton, the Discovery Channel picked up what was to be a series of documentaries and, with Steve at the forefront, the channel's Animal Planet went on to win a thrilled audience of literally hundreds of million subscribers in 160 countries.

'That he had an American wife meant it was a formula made in heaven,' John said. 'It was like when you make up a new formula for a soft drink. I knew from day one it was a success.'

Would Steve have become such a big hit without Terri? It was a question many people were to pose, but marketing or not, whoever was responsible for his international fame, nothing could take away from Steve his rapport with the wild, his uncanny knack of reading an animal's behaviour.

Mal Brough, whose son James and daughter Sarah work at Steve and Terri's Australia Zoo, as do literally hundreds of other people from around Queensland's Sunshine Coast, had some thoughts on who should get recognition for the conservationist's international profile. While recognising Steve's achievements, Mal told Australia's *Who* magazine: 'Without Terri, most of his life would have been what he was doing back then with his dad, collecting and marking and capturing rogue crocodiles.'

In fact, they complemented each other. What was more remarkable was this mutual love and respect was there for all to see. It also helped that the very attractive and photogenic Mrs Irwin was a perfect foil for her rugged husband. It is not trite to say that they seemed to have been made for each other.

Often, when I had dropped by at the zoo, I was told that Steve and Terri were away on a shoot. But it was never a case of grabbing an overnight bag and dashing off with a small cine camera. Flights had to be arranged, if the location was a long way off, 4WD vehicles rented, and a camera crew put together—to say nothing of arranging the transportation of their equipment. A game plan had to be drawn up: what was the best scenario, what was the worst? What was the weather going to be like? And so on. Medical equipment had to be checked in case of an injury, anti-venom packed, along with maps, spare batteries ... the list went on.

Despite the best preparations, however, the unexpected often occurred. Photographers have often moaned: 'Never work with children or animals—you can't keep them under control.'

Out in the wild, it was a lot tougher than in a studio.

7

A Man of Intellect

I get called an adrenaline junkie every other minute
and I'm just fine with that.

Danger, indeed death, was always lurking.

Once, on a trip into the Simpson Desert Terri herself came close to serious injury. She fell while climbing a rock face and was saved only from a long drop by the fact that she was tethered by a rope to Steve. But she badly scraped her skin against the rock and came close to falling further—and pulling Steve with her—until he was able to reach down and grab her wrist, hauling her to safety with superhuman strength. Terri was beginning to match Steve for scars and scratches!

As a husband and wife conservation team, the couple's fame was spreading. In 1994, two years into married life, they were advised that a large saltwater crocodile was causing concern at a popular fishing and camping area on the Normanby River in the Lakefield National Park. It needed to be relocated and Steve knew it was going to be quite a job—the reptile was estimated to be in the region of 5 metres (16 feet) long and had often approached people in fishing boats.

Sometimes it had caused several near heart attacks as it approached camp sites, yet it had made no attempt to attack anyone. Nicknamed Old Faithful, there were fears among rangers that he might be shot by illegal hunters who might decide to take it upon themselves to eliminate 'the nuisance.'

Steve was not to know it, but the Lakefield National Park would, 12 years later, be the last place in the bush he would visit before he died. For then, though, in 1994, his job was not to track but to trap—and then try a different system of dealing with a crocodile. Instead of catching it and relocating it—a difficult job with such a large reptile—his plan was to restrain it, then leave it where it was in a trap. It would then be harassed, a strategy designed to make the crocodile fear humans—instill into it what Steve described as 'people shyness'.

The crocodile was easy enough to spot, its eyes watching Steve and Terri's tin boat as they moved towards it in their small boat for a closer examination. The reptile taunted them by flaunting its vast bulk, finally dropping into the murky depths only after it had sparked their interest. With the help of a team from the zoo and park rangers, Steve set up two long, square-shaped wire mesh cages on the banks of the billabong, with a sizeable chunk of pork as bait inside them and a trap door ready to drop into place once the crocodile had gone in to take the meat. The trap had been set so that when the crocodile pulled at the meat it would release a bag of weights which, as it fell, would pull tight a rope around the entrance, rather like pulling on the drawstring of a pair of shorts.

On their first night the team caught one of the other crocs living in the waterhole, a female, which didn't interest Steve. He opened up the trap's entranceway and let her swim away.

The following night there was success. The big reptile they had been after was trapped and after a quick examination Steve decided it was the best-looking crocodile he had ever seen. But this was no beauty contest. It was time to get down to the business of scaring the crocodile so much that it would not worry visitors to the park again. It was a matter of being cruel to be kind.

He and Terri revved outboard motor engines near the trap, while from the shore a 4WD motor roared, an added noise attack. The sounds upset the crocodile, which was just what Steve wanted. He hoped his plan of making it afraid of humans and their equipment was beginning to work. The couple and their team set up their camp where the crocodile could see and smell them. Then throughout the night they continued to harass the creature by shining high-beam spotlights into its eyes.

Next, Steve fired several shots into the water near the crocodile. He was to say in his book that it broke his heart 'to subject the king of this territory to such extremes, but if he doesn't learn he will almost certainly be killed. If I can't teach him to stop approaching park visitors, Old Faithful, his family, and the entire ecosystem will be destroyed.'

There was one final exercise to be employed to ensure that the crocodile became afraid of humans: what Steve described as 'people power'. He, Terri and six friends and rangers hauled the crocodile onto the embankment and straddled him, pinning him down with their collective weight. Then everyone jumped back, allowing the croc to return to the water.

Steve's drastic measures worked. Returning to the waterhole months later, he found tracks indicating that the croc was still around but had not caused any concern to campers. Further checks later in the year revealed that Old Faithful was still in the area but had always slid quietly into the water whenever he heard a human approaching. What Steve needed to do next, he decided, was to keep preaching his message to humans—to learn to respect crocodiles and to try to understand them. The exercise involving Old Faithful had been captured on film, so Steve was able to use it to explain to the world what he had done, and why.

What has not been generally realised is that for all his showman-like performances for the camera, Steve took his conservation work so seriously that he wrote a number of zoological papers. So highly regarded was his expertise that much later the University of Queensland decided, before death intervened, Steve should be given an honourary professorship.

One of Steve's papers has been about the life and breeding habits of a large striped and spotted desert lizard known as a perentie. There is one living at the zoo which Steve collected in the Simpson Desert with Terri, bringing it back to mate with the females already living there. Part of his legacy has been to ensure that zoos around the world keep a healthy breeding program of the lizards so that their numbers can eventually be sustained in the desert.

As Steve's fame and knowledge spread, his detractors—those who had thought that he was little more than a hollow entertainer, a showman making animals perform for him and the cameras like a circus ringmaster—began to change their opinion. He knew as much about wild animals and their habitats as any other expert.

He was finding favour with such prestigious journals as *Scientific American*, which ran a long interview with him.

Steve Irwin was being taken seriously. Very seriously.

With Terri at his side, he constantly pushed home the point, as he had done with me, that it was vital to act now and save the vanishing wilderness. The couple explained it was sometimes difficult getting their message across in countries that had totally different cultures. They had worked in Fiji, for example, where some of the tribes they'd dealt with had no word for conservation and no concept of numbers above 100. So the couple agreed that as well as looking at the animals in their third-world projects, they also had to look at the people and their life styles and understand how they worked. The first rule in encouraging them to save their habitat, they suggested, was to ensure that the people had full bellies and healthy children. Then they could move on to educating people that animals were a 'cool thing' to be proud of instead of something to simply consume or make money out of.

'In 30 years time,' said Steve, 'those squeaky little crocodiles that we gave them are going to pay huge dividends.'

He also spoke about the neighbouring country of Indonesia 'where there seems to be such rapid habitat destruction.' But he and his team from Australia Zoo were working at saving any animals that were likely to become extinct because of habitat destruction. 'We're pulling them into zoos—predominantly rescuing the animals that are going to die anyway—and housing them, learning every single detail about how we can breed them and establishing satellite colonies of that species, so that we're ready when the cure does come, when we can rebuild habitat.' All of the good zoos in the world were taking regional approaches and, he said, 'those that aren't doing it need to pick up their act or get out.' Zoos had to be educational facilities with the ability to put animals back in the wild.

With every opportunity she had, Terri heaped praise on her husband and his team. She reflected as she spoke to *Scientific American* on what I had often thought—that there were people in the academic arena who were brilliant at what they did, but were as 'boring as the day is long'. She made the point that 'you would never sit down and watch a lecture from any of them if you are a football fan, if you like watching *Melrose Place*, if you tune into your regular soap opera every day, if you think Jacques Cousteau is still alive— because you don't know anything about documentaries. These are the kind of people that, by default, we are reaching.'

They were reaching them not only through Steve's brilliance but that of their support team. 'You've heard of a Spielberg production?' Terri asked. 'You know what a Stainton production is? A John Stainton production is real,' she said of Steve's manager, producer and director. 'It's not a rubber crocodile. It's a guy out in the bush and he goes, "I think there is a koala around here that needs help." And he'll find a baby koala 69 foot up a telephone pole somewhere … I have never before or since seen anybody in my life with this gift for wildlife. So the fact that he [an academic] publishes and sits out and does field study and that he knows the Latin name of everything is boring. And this eight-year-old kid who's keen on animals doesn't give a rip about any of that. So what we've found is that the television shows are appealing to these people, and Steve happens to make a great role model.'

At every opportunity they preached their message about their zoo animals and why they were there—not so that people could just look at them, take a photo, and then wander off without learning anything. What they wanted to do was educate not just the zoo visitors but the world into understanding animals. They wanted children and adults to understand animals instead of trying to destroy them. Instead of—as Terri put it—'just going whack, whack, whack and killing it' people were now interested in animals because they were reaching kids, reaching new generations, reaching people who once didn't give a damn about wildlife or conservation.

No other animal held such a special place in Steve's heart as the crocodile. Except, perhaps elephants—and Harriet. Harriet was a special tortoise who died at the ripe old age of 175 in mid-2006. What a big-time Crocodile Hunter finds so appealing in a simple tortoise might be cause for wonder—except that Harriet was no ordinary tortoise. I first came face to face with her—really face-to-face—in 2000 when she was celebrating her 170th birthday.

'Steve makes sure she gets the very best treatment,' one of Harriet's keepers at the zoo told me while the conservationist was away with Terri working on a documentary. 'Whenever he calls in every day or so he makes a special point of asking about Harriet.'

In 2005 I was back. One hundred and seventy five years of age and still going strong Harriet, acquired by the Irwin family from another reptile park in 1987, was breaking all records for tortoise longevity. What a story Steve's hard-shelled friend could have told if only she could speak.

Purported to be the oldest living creature on the planet, Harriet could have told us a few things about the history of the world if she could only speak—and given the evolutionary theories of Charles Darwin, who first found her on the island of Galapagos way back in the 1800s, her descendants might well end up with that ability.

If truth be told, visiting Harriet was rather like dropping in on a maiden aunt. On the shy side—it took a while to coax the old girl out of her shell—she didn't do much apart from pretending to be a large rock, eating zuchini, carrots and eggplant, and walking around at half a mile an hour. Sometimes Steve would pop into her pen to pose with her for the tourists, but for most of her days she was content to just sit about with her private memories. It was the weight of history that she carried on her enormous back, so to speak, that made Harriet such a drawcard for tourists of every nationality.

After all, she'd been around since well before the old sailing ships were chopped up for firewood and man put his feet on the moon.

Cameras clicked, videos recorded and children who were dwarfed by the 23-stone giant Galapagos tortoise, (geochelone nigra porteri) stared wide-eyed as she enjoyed her 'constitutional' around her pen when I called by during what was otherwise a typically busy day at Steve and Terri's zoo. Harriet had found the secret of long,

long life but surely it was not just a diet of eggplant or Steve's tender loving care?

'That's got a lot to do with it, but it's probably lifestyle and genes,' said her keeper, Richard Jackson. 'She's not under any pressure, she goes at her own steady pace—no jerky movements—doesn't burn up any energy at all and is loved by everybody. She's in absolutely perfect health and we reckon she's good to reach 200.

'Don't let those watery eyes fool you into thinking she's sad. All those tears are a natural protection from her place of origin, where there was a lot of volcanic ash flying around. And don't worry about her missing teeth—she never had any in the first place. She has a hidden beak to munch up her food.'

Of course, there were no concerns about keeping a roof over her head. Harriet carried her home with her—that huge, solar-powered heat-retaining shell which took up half her weight—wherever she wandered, although she did also have a heated cave for cold winter nights.

We don't know if she dreamed, but there would have been a lot of life to look back over if she did ...

She would have seen the 20-year-old English scientist Charles Darwin sailing in to her island of Santa Cruz in 1831 on board his ship HMS *Beagle* a year after she had been hatched and she'd recall how, four years later, she and two other tortoises, named Tom and Dick, found themselves on board the *Beagle* heading for England as subjects for scientific research.

While Darwin was impressing the world with his theory of evolution, he wasn't too hot on the sexing of tortoises, it seemed, and believing Harriet was a male, named her Harry. Anyway, the three names, Tom, Dick and Harry, had a nice ring about them.

Harriet's capture probably saved her from a terrible fate, for the Galapagos island tortoises were targeted by merchant sailors who collected them for food on their journeys. Tortoises could live for a year without food of their own, which did away with the need for sailors to preserve meat.

At the time of 'Harry's' voyage back to England, Queen Victoria was just a teenager and King George IV had been succeeded to the throne by William IV, a man who himself enjoyed life at a tortoise's pace, indulging in quiet conversation and peaceful walks. Morse, meanwhile, was still working on his electric telegraph.

The cold weather of England left the three tortoises rather shell-shocked and the lack of sunshine reduced them to virtual year-round hibernation. Even Darwin could not fail to have noticed that any more exposure to English weather would end evolution for his tortoises there and then.

By chance, John Wickham, a first lieutenant on HMS *Beagle* with Darwin, was offered a job as police magistrate in Australia and he offered to take Tom, Dick and Harry with him to save them from certain death in a British blizzard. So back across the world they sailed, arriving in Brisbane in 1842, a year before Charles Dickens' novel *A Christmas Carol* was published.

The three herbivores lived for a time at Old Government House in Brisbane before being moved in 1860, strapped down on the back of a horse and cart, to the Botanic Gardens. There, despite Australia's Gold Rush still keeping thousands in the goldfields, they became creatures of intense curiosity, with people travelling from around the country to gaze at them, sketch them and sit their children on their backs for a free but rather slow walk around the park.

Five years later, when 'Harry' reached the age of 35, the world was shocked at the news of the assassination of American President Abraham Lincoln. Historic events were being created around the tortoise and its two friends as it contentedly munched its greens in the gardens.

Three years on, the last boatload of convicts from Britain arrived in Australia, another historical landmark, but there were many more to come in the life of the fascinating creature from the Galapagos Islands. Around the time that 'Harry' reached his 50th birthday in 1880 jailers were leading notorious outlaw Ned Kelly to the gallows in the Old Melbourne Jail. Could the tortoise hear the cheers in the nearby streets two years later, in 1882, when Australia beat England at cricket on home soil for the first time, giving birth to the Ashes?

Old age finally caught up with Dick and he died under a palm tree one sunny afternoon in the late 1880s, leaving 'Harry' and Tom, now the equivalent of pensioners, to become part of the celebrations in 1901 when their adopted country became unified and the Australian flag fluttered for the first time. They lived on through the two wars until Tom passed away in 1949. Alone and probably fretting over the death of the long-term mate, 'Harry' was still wandering through the gardens at the age of 123 in 1953 when Queen Elizabeth II was crowned in Westminster Abbey.

'His' back daubed with paint by soldiers and sailors who had written their names to mark their visit to the gardens, Harry remained in the best of health until it was decided he should be moved on to a fauna reserve on the Gold Coast, south of Brisbane. There, in 1960, a visiting director from Hawaii's Honolulu Zoo made a discovery that startled the tortoise's keepers. Harry was a 'she'. So, Harriet was born—or rather, started life officially as a female after 130 years.

The clues were there, though, long before. When a keeper put a female in with 'Harry' years before there was a tremendous fight in the night and the next morning the new arrival was found on her back, swinging her legs helplessly in the air. Harriet, not at all happy to be sharing her space with another female, had delivered the reptile equivalent of a 'cat fight.'

Australia's stars—Dame Edna Everage and Kylie Minogue—were created or born when Harriet reached her 126th and 138th birthdays.

She was 132 when Steve was born.

There were the 2000 Olympics, the attacks on America a year later, the exploration of space ... Harriet lived through the best and the worst of our times. Still she plodded on, walking into history daily.

She made it into the *Guinness Book of World Records* sharing the honours with a—by then deceased—Madagascar radiated tortoise called Tui Malila, presented to the Tongan royal family by Captain James Cook in the late 1700s, and which was around 190 when it died. But Harriet was still alive and, sort of kicking. Even her keepers were in awe.

'Just think about it,' said keeper Richard Jackson as he prepared for yet another of Harriet's birthday parties. 'One and three quarter centuries ago, or thereabouts, she was on a boat heading for England, a long time before cars, phones or television. What she must have seen, what she could tell us if only she could.'

In recognition of the amazing creature's life, her story was preserved in the pages of a children's book, *Darwin's Tortoise*. As for Darwin, perhaps he had already guessed that his 'Harry' was destined for a very long life when he said: '...whilst this planet has gone cycling on according to the fixed law of gravity, from so simple a beginning endless forms most beautiful and most wonderful have been, and are being, evolved.'

'You know,' said one of the zoo visitors during the birthday celebrations, 'it's a curious thing when you think that Harriet was found by a Darwin and in her old age she'll be seen out by an Irwin. Their names have a certain ring about them, don't you think?'

Sadly Harriet died from heart failure in June, 2006, three months before her beloved owner Steve met his death. But he'd told everyone while Harriet was still alive that he wished he could live to a ripe old age like her.

'I'd love to live until I'm 80,' he said. 'I want to see my daughter grow up; I want to love my wife. I hope I live a long and healthy life but if I don't, I've had such a wonderful, fulfilled life and I get what a lot of other people don't get, which is to educate people about conservation. There's my reason for living, my passion. This is why God created me.'

8

Bindi is Introduced to a Snake

*I believe our biggest issue is the same biggest issue that the whole
world is facing and that's habitat destruction.*

When Steve and Terri teamed up, Harriet was one of the first
exhibits he proudly showed her. Years later, when Terri was pregnant
with their first child, Bindi, they decided to take a break from crocodile, snake and lizard hunting and pay a visit to none other than
Harriet's former home, the Galapagos Islands.

It would certainly be Terri's last chance to travel overseas on a
documentary shoot before she became a mother and nothing was
going to stop her. She was determined to see the place where the
famous old tortoise had originated. It turned out to be yet another
'trip of a lifetime', their cameras turning on a mixed population of
iguanas, sea lions, and tortoises. Steve's manager and the documentary director and producer, John Stainton made sure that Terri was
well cared for in her delicate state, providing ice packs on the catamaran they had hired so she could place them on her stomach to
keep cool in the stifling conditions. By the time they returned to

Australia they had learned much about Harriet's distant relatives.

There was, and is, of course much more at the zoo to enthrall visitors than Harriet and Steve's other great loves, the crocodiles. Almost as soon as visitors enter the grounds they find themselves staring into a pen where injured birds are recovering. They've been hit by cars or attacked by cats and dogs but under the care of the zoo staff they have been nursed back to good health. Those able to fly again have been released; those unable to return to the wild are assured of a good home for the rest of their lives. There's a 5000-seat Animal Planet Crocoseum where 'birds fly overhead, the snakes slither around,' says the zoo's website.

Steve made sure that his zoo was stocked with mainly Australian creatures—echidnas, kangaroos, crocodiles of course, possums and wombats, many of which can be fed by visitors. There are also animals that can't be found in the wild in Australia—the Asian elephants and Sumatran and Bengal tigers as well as alligators. 'Tigers,' said Steve, 'are highly endangered in the wild and they're at the zoo because we've started a breeding program.'

Then the Irwins were into their very own personal breeding program when into the world on 24 July, 1998 came Bindi Sue, whose name was derived from a crocodile called Bindi that Steve worked with—fearsome Graham's girlfriend, in fact—and Sui, the family dog. Steve was present at the birth.

In hardly no time at all the proud new parents were making the decision to take Bindi with them when they went off on a previously-planned day assignment to film sea turtles. So at the age of six—six days that is!—Bindi was part of the team, a sleepy part, who spent the day on the documentary shoot.

Less than two weeks later, Bindi was off with her parents again, this time to America for a film shoot in Texas. It was straight into an adventure, for, having been dropped at a remote air strip in a national park, they found there was no pre-arranged rental car there, or anyone for that matter. Heavy rains had prevented the car being delivered and it looked like the Irwins, their daughter and the film crew were destined for a long night in the middle of nowhere. Fortunately a man drove by with a pick-up truck and he was able to fit them all in and take them to some accommodation.

Steve's plan, as crazy as ever, was to find some rattlesnakes—the bigger the better for the cameras. When they entered a ruined homestead they found themselves face to face with two snakes, which Steve quickly declared were not venomous. It surprised Terri that he was able to make such an assessment, considering he was not accustomed to the reptiles of America. Fortunately, his appraisal turned out to be correct. Within a short time, and to the Irwins' amazement, baby Bindi was reaching out to touch one. Their hearts thumped with excitement—she was showing all the signs of being a true child of the wild!

Steve decided on their return to Australia there was no further time to lose in introducing his daughter to every animal in the zoo. He carried her around on a conducted tour and soon she had met them all but one—a boa constrictor.

When I heard that Steve would soon be introducing Bindi to the huge snake I told him I'd love to be in on the act to record the moment for posterity. He agreed and I duly turned up at the zoo where Steve and Terri chatted excitedly about their recent trip to America and their plans to raise Bindi and perhaps other children who might come along, in a family that loved and cared for animals.

It was the first time I'd met Steve face to face. Of course, he was fitted in his trademark khakis, a bit of mud on his face, grime in his fingernails, a strong handshake. His eyes were darting everywhere around the zoo grounds before we stepped into a nearby office. He was a bundle of energy and I could understand why people thought

above: Steve was given his first snake, a python, when he was seven.

below: A toss of his head: Steve was always going to be different.

opposite page, top: Among Steve's teenage sports was spear fishing. opposite page, below left: Not content with catching monster fish, Steve preferred to dodge croc teeth. opposite page, below right: His mother, who often helped him handle crocs at the zoo, was 'Mother Nature' to him. above: Wrestling crocs was child's play. below: It was a pleasant change to feel fur against his face, instead of a croc's scales.

Surfing was one of Steve's great loves.

Putting the seal on a great love affair. Steve and Terri at their wedding.

above: Steve and Terri share a meaningful look during an interview in Los Angeles, in 2002.

below: Steve proudly shows off some babies in his family: son Bob, daughter Bindi and a young croc.

'Bring 'em on!' Snakes of all types were no challenge for Steve.

top: Harriet the ancient tortoise was one of Steve and Terri's favourites at the Australia Zoo. *above:* Bindi gets to know snakes at a very young age.

opposite page, top: George Bush chats with Steve and Terri at a VIP function in Canberra in 2003. *opposite page, below:* Steve introduces US television host Jay Leno to one of his slippery friends.

top: Making a spectacle of himself with Dame Edna Everage.
above: Prime Minister John Howard plays father figure with Bindi while her dad is distracted at a function.
opposite page: Danger zone: Steve feeds a croc while daughter Bindi clings on.

Steve creates a storm as he holds baby Bob while feeding a croc.

above: Steve's launch, *Croc One*, moored at Port Douglas after his death.
below: Steve poses by a crocodile trap with Bindi and his father, Bob, in the Lakefield National Park shortly before his death.

left: Stingrays have been described as the 'pussycats of the sea'.
below: A stingray barb, similar to one that pierced Steve's heart.

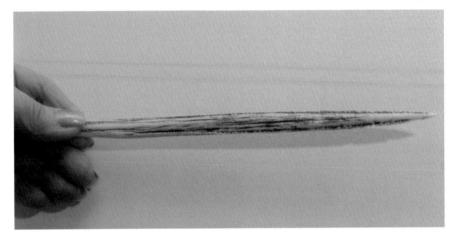

opposite page, top: Shocked fans laid flowers all around the walls of Australia Zoo after Steve's death.
opposite page, below: Grief-stricken: close friend and manager John Stainton, Terri, son Bob and Steve's father, Bob Irwin, at his memorial service.

following page: An image the world will never forget: eight-year-old Bindi pays tribute to her father, 'my hero', at his memorial service.

that he was hyperactive. He was up every morning at 3.30 am, ready to go to work because the last thing he wanted was to be still in bed when his charges greeted the dawn.

He didn't smoke and did not drink coffee because, as Terri once explained, 'if he did that he'd blow his head off because he's so wired'. In fact, she had told her friends at the zoo several times that she was worried about his health because he was so full of non-stop energy and the demands on him physically were enormous. She wasn't worried about his mind, even though he slept for only four hours a night. It was the risks he took with his body, despite his apparent strength.

'He's like an Olympic athlete,' she once told television interviewer Andrew Denton. 'You know, if an orang-outang is 60 feet up a tree, he's got to climb the tree and hang out with the orang-outang. If there's something down in the river, he's got to just swim through the rapids and he, he's always getting very hurt. Well, it is a worry.'

'Thing is, mate,' said Steve at our zoo meeting, 'I do get bashed around, but it doesn't matter to me. Unless we do something quickly about teaching kids about our dying animals there isn't going to be much left, if anything, for the generations that follow. The way we're going we're experiencing in evolution terms the beginning of the end. There's one big word that we've all got to get into our heads and make sure it stays there. It's "awareness". We've got to be aware of what's happening around us and if we see something that worries us, we've got to do something about it.

'Okay, what I'm aware of is the destruction of land where our wild animals live. It's all disappearing and they're losing their homes. What I want to do, with the help of others who share my vision, is to buy up land and save it for the animals that are losing their environment nearby. Just move them into my bit of space. It's a small token in terms of the big wide world but hey, we've got to do something. If all the big businesses in every country bought up land for the animals we might be able to save a lot of them that are facing extinction.

'But we've also got to stop the wanton killing. If somebody hits an animal with a car they've got to stop and go and help it, not just leave it there to die because it could be the mate of the last pair of wombats or possums or whatever living in that particular place and if that one dies it will be the end of a partnership and the end of a new line. This isn't rocket science, mate. We've got to stop being so bloody selfish. We're not the only ones on this planet.'

Interestingly, I did not feel that I was being lectured. I was listening to a man whose heart was filled with passion. His words were simple enough, but their meaning was powerful. I thought again of brilliant academics who were extremely well-versed in their chosen subjects, yet had no means of communicating their knowledge in a way that ordinary people could understand. There was no jargon in Steve Irwin's words. He said it straight from the heart and it was basic and it was easy.

Terri wandered off to get the baby as Steve told of his plans. 'The message is through television,' he said. 'Everybody watches television and if I can get myself on the box educating people about our wonderful world then at least I'll be doing something. Terri's a great inspiration. She's taken to everything like a duck to water—' and he laughed at the analogy he, the animal man, had drawn.

He was almost childlike with his infectious enthusiasm and it was true that some of his friends had described him as like a young boy who had never grown up. Yet he was clearly highly intelligent and totally at one with the environment. He was a self-made cultural icon who, despite his rawness, could rub shoulders with anybody.

Bruce Willis rang him one day in 2001 after watching some of the *Crocodile Hunter* series. 'Look, I love you guys,' said Willis 'I sit down with my daughters to see your show whenever I can. I even watch it in my trailer when I'm through for the day filming a movie. What you've done is great. If you have a message that you want out, there's nothing more powerful than the big screen.'

Steve was to find that out later when Willis helped produce Steve's 2002 film, *The Crocodile Hunter Collision Course*. Terri got in on the act then, saying in an interview to promote the film: 'The amazing thing about Steve is that he's the real deal—a sensitive man of ethics, integrity and willingness to lay his life on the line for what he believes in.'

Which is what Steve told me as we waited for Terri to bring Bindi back so he could introduce the baby to the boa.

'Look at all this,' he said, lifting up that khaki shirt of his to reveal a torso pockmarked with small scars, a nip here, a scratch there, a bite, a claw, a fang. 'Just little pink bits,' was one of his favourite ways of brushing off the damage whenever anyone remarked.

I'd seen photos of Steve with blood on his face and arms after a non-toxic snake sank its fangs into him and here in the flesh was a whole new—or perhaps they were old—collection of wounds. 'It's what people like to see and I don't care as long as it gets the message over,' he said. 'I've been bitten, mauled, scratched, but that goes with the territory. It shouldn't make people afraid of wild animals because I often have to take them full on for their own benefit. All I want is for people to understand them and to see there's nothing to be afraid of if they just leave them alone, just let them be and don't try to interfere with their lives. I don't care whether people say I'm a showman, an adrenaline junkie, whatever. They can send me up, shoot me down, I don't care as long as people listen to what I say.'

Steve's critics have said he interfered with animals just for the sake of the camera. Shortly after his death, British producer Ray Mears, whose television programs include *Extreme Survival*, said he believed that television's demands for sensation had pushed Steve to be too daring, putting safety to one side for the sake of drama.

'He clearly took a lot of risks and television encouraged him to do that,' he said. 'It's a shame television audiences need that to be attracted to wildlife. Dangerous animals, you leave them alone because they will defend themselves. Nature defends itself.'

We walked, the three of us—the Irwins leading the way with the baby—from Steve's office to meet the boa constrictor. 'This,' said Steve, 'is one of our friendliest—' and before I could move he'd draped it around my neck. That is when he uttered those words which I'd never forgotten: 'Crikey, don't show it you're afraid. That's the worst thing you can do.'

Then he relieved me of the snake and draped it around his own neck. He took Bindi into his arms, held the snake by the neck and gently brushed its mouth against Bindi's face. He struck a statue-like pose, eyes staring, teeth flashing, as I raised my camera. It was too much 'over the top' I felt. I could hear my picture editor saying: 'Too posed, old boy.'

'Can you just relax a bit more, Steve?' I implored. But he found it difficult. Every time I aimed the camera at him it was as if a cerebral computer forced him to adopt a frozen pose, a living photo-graph before he'd become a photograph.

As we made our way back to his office for a further chat I realised that this was all part of the grand show. He had spent so many years in front of cameras and seen how he'd come across as a more relaxed figure and decided that the 'perfect pose' was the way to go. It might have worked for the covers of glossy magazine but I felt unhappy about it. In journalistic terms, I liked his words but not his pictures.

'Just tell me again, Steve, why you did that with the snake and the baby,' I said.

'Simple mate—the sooner she learns about every creature, the less fear she's going to have. In time, when she's old enough to understand, I'll tell her all about them. She'll learn from me at a very early age what to be concerned about, what to feel okay about. Just wait, you'll see she'll grow up to be a bloody good little kid, if for no other reason than that she's my daughter.'

How accurate that prediction was to be. But then, he should have known. After all, he had his own first confrontation with a crocodile as a child, although he was nine years older than baby Bindi.

Steve had been born into relatively poor circumstances but by the first couple of years of the new millennium, he was on his way to riches, thanks to his and Terri's documentaries. But very little went into his pocket. He and Terri began buying up tracts of wilderness to save them from developers. In Australia alone they bought some 16,000ha (35,000 acres), but there were reports—that he had also purchased land in the Pacific islands of Vanuatu and Fiji as well as the United States. John Stainton was to deny this, but even so the reports persisted. In any case, all Steve and Terri collected was a salary from the zoo, like everyone else employed there. All the rest of the money, running into millions of dollars, from the documentaries and the film, the merchandise, videos, shows, sponsorship, was put into the preservation of the planet's wildlife.

'To say that I've got millions in the bank, mate, would be a load of crap,' he said, even though I hadn't got around to asking him about those reports. 'Of course I've made money but it's all gone back into wildlife welfare. I don't keep it.'

There had been estimates that he was earning $A4 million a year from Australia Zoo alone, to say nothing of his television work that was netting him $A20 million a year. No, he insisted, he didn't put it all away in the bank. But the income was a reflection on the success his publicity was achieving. Three years after my meeting with Steve, *Business Review Weekly* magazine estimated that his and Stainton's earnings peaked at $A16.3 million in 2001. A year later the two men made it onto the magazine's list of highest paid Australian entertainers in the category of 'highest placed newcomer', stepping in at number five.

'It's no good being a conservationist and keeping your lips sealed tight, no matter what you might be doing physically,' he told me as he admitted he had made 'good money' which was his aim because it was required for his wildlife work. 'You've got to tell people what you're doing so they'll pick it up, too, do the same thing.

'As for me, I'm going to keep on doing this until I can't do it any more, and that will be the day when I say goodbye to this world. I'm not going to change course in mid-stream. Steve Irwin will keep up the struggle for the creatures that live on this planet of ours because the trend is to destroy, not preserve.

'Do you know that crocodiles are our oldest living dinosaurs—they've been around for millions of years and here we are close to wiping them out because we're taking away their space, shooting them and showing our fear of them. We need some understanding here. There's something wrong when we put houses up near their habitat and then say "Hey, there's a croc at the end of the garden, we'd better get rid of it or it will eat us." Simple solution, leave them to their space and go and find somewhere else to live.

'I can't tell you the number of times I've heard comments like "there's a croc, we have to kill it," or "the only good shark is a dead one". We freeze at the sight of a snake and look for something to beat the living daylights out of it with. We stamp on spiders. What right do we have to do these things? Why do we do these things? Killing a spider isn't going to make them go away, at least not in the immediate instance although in time we'll be hearing "whatever happened to spiders?" just as we're already beginning to ask "whatever happened to all the butterflies?"

'We're spreading houses into all areas of the rainforests. Our wild animals are running out of space. Habitat destruction, mate, it's the worst kind of cruelty. Possums and koalas aren't climbing over people's fences because they want to pay a social call on people who live there. It's because the houses have gone up where they've always lived. Down there in New South Wales around Coffs Harbour, you've got koalas ending up in people's swimming pools because houses have gone up on the old tracks they've been using.

'Some people have to leave ropes dangling over the edge of the pool into the water in case a koala falls in and can then drag itself out. What kind of life is that for these poor little creatures? Leaving ropes in swimming pools so koalas can get out. And we're slaughtering them on the roads all the time. It's a disgrace. One day, and it will be a long way away but in terms of evolution not so long, there wouldn't be any animals left if we go on the way we are.'

As we chatted, staff came and went, butting in to ask Steve about aspects of the zoo. It was clear from the comfortable way he and staff members spoke to one another that he was an easy-going and much-liked boss.

Steve revealed that he had plans to set up his own koala sanctuary soon. They were animals that needed very special care, for one single koala required the leaves of 300 gum trees each year. 'We're killing everything. They want to cull this and cull that. They say there's too many kangaroos and that may be the case but then there's talk of farming them to be eaten. I reckon that's a shocker, mate. They're already farming emus. The roo and the emu are on our coat of arms and people have forgotten that and are just intent on eating them. It's a disgrace.'

Steve ran a hand through his shock of blond hair and blew air from bulging cheeks. He was exasperated. Habitat destruction was a topic he returned to several times and he emphasised it wasn't just happening in his native Australia. He spoke of the trees that were being chopped down in Indonesia and Malaysia, where natural forest had been cut down to make way for palm-oil. Big birds that used to land on the old jungle trees now couldn't land on the flimsy, flapping fronds of the palms. They flew off looking for somewhere else—but there wasn't much left, he said.

'You know, the basic problem is greed and poverty. The poor chop down trees because they need wood for fire and big companies chop them down for profit, with corrupt officials getting their take while looking the other way, before the wood is exported or sold to local factories. No-one thinks about the wildlife that is being left homeless or destroyed due to this desperation and this greed.'

I said goodbye to Steve on the day that he'd introduced his daughter to a python, the first time anyone had seen him do it. We'd catch up again some day, he said. Yes, I told him, but it won't be beside a croc-filled billabong.

9

Crikey! Movie Star Status

My dad taught me from my youngest childhood memories through these connections with Aboriginal and tribal people that you must always protect people's sacred status, regardless of the past.

Some years later, the fearlessness that Steve hoped he had instilled into Bindi came back to bite him—or rather her—when she was bitten on the lip by a non-poisonous snake. She had come to love snakes so when they saw a large carpet python sliding across the road one night she told her father she wanted it.

Steve picked it up and handed it to her, warning that it was a 'bit bitey.' Cuddling the snake, she started singing 'Rock-a-bye-baby' when it suddenly struck out and bit her on the lip. She told him she was okay but then it bit her on the nose, causing blood to flow. She suffered no ill effects, but some people wondered whether growing up with snakes and becoming so closely bonded with them had taken away too much of her natural wariness and left her too exposed to danger. Steve did not think so. He said simply that he was very proud of her.

In all of his television interviews he pushed the message that not only did he love all the animals in the zoo, he was as happy as any father could be.

As he sat on a plane returning from a documentary shoot in Africa in 1999, John Stainton was struck with a brilliant idea: he would write a script for a Hollywood-style movie, starring Steve and Terri as themselves. On his return to Australia his enthusiasm for the project grew, especially when, as expected, the Irwins said they could hardly wait to get started.

'But they aren't actors!' many who heard of the initial proposal cried. But John knew how he was going to make it work—using Steve and Terri as the kingpins, going about their work in the outback, while setting a story using actors around them. It was, in fact, an amazing story that was so much at odds with the image the world had of the couple … .Steve and Terri are suspected by the CIA of stealing high-security data after an American government spy satellite comes down in the crocodile-infested Australian tropics.

At stake is the future of the world, so the CIA sends two of its most respected undercover operatives Down Under to find the satellite's black box. Steve and Terri are hunted by the agents, but remain unaware as they go about their business of catching and relocating a rogue crocodile. When they find out they are being followed, they believe the agents are nothing more than crocodile poachers.

The Crocodile Hunter: Collision Course was to be John's first feature film but he knew he could pull it off, crossing documentary shots with drama. It was a delicate balance. 'I wanted the CIA plot to be complex enough to keep Steve's world looking simplistic, and I wanted the other players in the movie to be like cardboard cut-out characters so the audience had no other focus but on Steve and Terri. I think it works,' he explained.

One of the film's stars—and an Australian favourite—Magda Szubanksi, who had worked with animals on the *Babe* films and her Australian television series *Dogwoman*, was keen to work with Steve. 'I think he's fascinating and really smart,' she said in the production notes. 'I've done a bit of stuff around animals now and I just find I love it. I find animal behaviour fascinating and I like people who like animals. And Steve loves animals; even the really challenging ones.'

Another Australian star eager to work with Steve was multi-award-winning Sydney actor David Wenham. The script appealed to him because it was very funny, there was a chance to work with Magda, one of the nation's greatest comic talents—and then, of course, there was Steve. Here, he said, was the opportunity to appear in a film with the Crocodile Hunter: 'Somebody who's achieved legendary status around the world and somebody who, I must say, is an extremely enigmatic and funny character up there on the screen. I think Steve Irwin is amazing.'

John Stainton realised there might be problems bringing professional actors together with a professional man of the wild and those difficulties did occur—mainly because Steve was so enthusiastic about his environment.

'A couple of the actors had to do scenes with Steve and it was probably a little daunting because Steve isn't an actor,' said John when he was interviewed about the movie. 'So he doesn't hit marks like they do and he ad-libs and he'll say what he wants to say about the snake or the crocodile or whatever. So for an actor to come into his world was like throwing somebody into the fire. They had to improvise a little bit, but they coped with it very well.'

As for Steve, he had more fun than he could have imagined. Stunts involved him standing on the top of moving trucks, falling out of trees and taking fake punches. He said, 'It was a stack of fun and the stunt crew'—who guided him—'was very strict and careful.

They planned and schemed and plotted for weeks. They grilled me on how much climbing I'd done, checking me out to see if I was a risk. But I'm in the vertical rescue team for the State Emergency Service. I climb trees to cut koala leaves virtually every other day. The Glasshouse Mountains? I grew up in 'em. My mum always used to say, "If you can't find him down, look up." So climbing a truck at 80 kilometres an hour was no problem.'

There were explosions, a fight on top of an overturned boat on top of a moving truck, and dashes through the Queensland undergrowth, all of which Steve took in his stride. Even though he and Terri jokingly admitted they were now Hollywood-style actors, they welcomed this novel way of getting their message about sustainable wildlife conservation across on the big silver screen.

Steve lived his passion for the wild daily, so that while other cast members lunched or took breaks, he was frequently to be seen hand in hand with little Bindi exploring the surrounding landscape.

He found her ants and spiders and delighted her with stories about their habitat and habits. Bindi was like a sponge, showing an interest in everything around her. He only hoped the film they were making would entertain and instruct the cinema audience in the same way.

'This is going to be the greatest conservation message the world has seen,' he said. While he mistakenly identifies the CIA agents in the film as poachers, he pointed out that in real life in parts of Australia there was a large trade in crocodile skins. 'That's something Terri and I fight vehemently to stop. I say there's no difference between skinning a crocodile and skinning a koala. They're native Australian wildlife and should be protected, not worn as some kind of garment.'

In the film set interviews, Terri became equally vociferous. 'If people can find love and sympathy and empathy and compassion for a crocodile, then we've got hope for saving just about anything. That's the object of the game. Over the years, Steve's gotten the feedback that the only good snake is a dead snake. Now we're finding people are responding with love for vultures as well as eagles, crocodiles, as well as koalas and the whole planet is really changing.'

'We're wildlife warriors,' said Steve, 'and we're training our daughter to be a wildlife warrior. Like any warrior, our job is to get out there and fight for wildlife.'

Because there's a golden rule among photographers and cinematographers to 'never work with children or animals' because they were traditionally unpredictable, Steve's knowledge was invaluable when it came to filming the creatures that were the wildlife stars. He told the camera operators that there would probably not be a second chance to shoot a particular scene—'get the first take, or you've missed it,' he would tell them.

He was also determined to ensure that none of the animals they used were placed under any stress. Kangaroos, spiders and snakes were taken onto the set for what might be several takes so Steve kept a watchful eye on them, insisting he be present at every scene involving wildlife to ensure they were not distressed. To ensure the humans were not hurt, too. Such a testing time came in one scene, when a large bird-eating spider, whose venom is very toxic to humans, was brought into the act to crawl up Terri's leg as she was driving the Irwins' truck.

'She only had a set of khakis between her and those fangs,' Steve said. 'They've got pretty big fangs which could certainly penetrate through the material, so I was watching the spider closely to see it wasn't going to drive its fangs through the khakis and hook into Terri's leg. So when I was happy it was going to do what we wanted and Terri was happy and the spider was happy, bang, we did it! It may look really risky, but in essence there's no risk because we understand the posturing of the spider. When you see it on the screen you will be interested to know it's Terri's leg.'

In another scene, Steve had to dangle a deadly brown snake. 'When I was doing the king brown snake, it opened its mouth and it swung past me and that was my cue. I saw that snake was starting to get stressed. He was getting aggressive enough to bite. So it was time to put him in a bag and take him away. He'd had enough.'

It meant delaying the scene but when Steve said a snake had had enough, they were words of wisdom that the rest of the cast and crew took to heart.

She may have been speaking about her husband, but Terri said: 'It's a real honour to be working with someone who'll lay his life on the line to defend wildlife. I think it's very exciting to take that kind of flavour into the movies. It's very exciting and very real.'

The film received mixed reviews from the critics and the audience. A number of Irwin fans did not think the movie was so very different from Steve's real-life adventures in his documentaries. Wrote one fan: 'I was expecting Steve [playing himself] would be encountering situations not found on his television show and his reaction to these events would provide the comedy. Nope; the first half of the movie plays (for the most part) like an expanded episode of his show.'

Steve saw such observations as positive. It meant that his documentaries were as powerful as any make-believe action movie. With much of the film work behind them, they set about plans for expanding the zoo. They were exciting times. Success followed them from project to project.

But in 2000 the joyful mood embracing Steve's family had been suddenly thrown into deep gloom when he received devastating news. His beloved mother had been killed in a car crash. Tears poured down his face as he recalled the wonderful times they had had together. The pain of losing her, he was to tell his many fans in a message posted on the Internet later, was 'unbearable and relentless'.

Steve and Terri then became parents a second time. Robert (Bob) was born in December 2003, and, while he was overwhelmed at the birth, Steve was devastated that his mother could not share his delight. He was inspired to write a personal tribute to her at the time—a tribute he wanted to share, along with photographs of Lyn, with his worldwide fans.

'My daughter Bindi came in one door as you went out another,' he said of his mother. 'My son baby Bob will never know you—here is real, fair dinkum pain. You come to me in my dreams; your spirit is with every wedge tailed eagle; I feel your breath in the westerly wind, but most of all I see your genes in my princess Bindi and my baby boy Bob …

'I loved my mum more than anything in the world. She nurtured, protected and loved me all my life. Lyn Irwin was a true "Australian Pioneer Woman", who dedicated her entire life to the rehabilitation and conservation of both the wildlife and to her family. Every single day she worked and toiled to save injured and orphaned joeys while maintaining a happy, healthy Irwin clan.'

His emotional tribute continued: 'You worked with me for 38 years to help me become the man I am today. You suckled me, changed my nappy, packed me off to school, blessed me with a career that is my whole life, cried with me when my pet snake died, belted me with your shoe when I was really naughty, fought for me, protected me, pushed me forward when the going got tough and raised me to fight for the preservation of wildlife until the day I die.

'I've adopted your strength, your passion and enthusiasm, your dedication and commitment, and will honour your presence by continuing to push forward as hard and fast as I possibly can, to ensure the survival of precious wildlife, the wilderness, and in essence, the human race. For without fresh water, trees, animals, and ecosystems, the world we know would not support human life; it would be an ugly, awful place. The spirit of Lynette Leslie Irwin, Lyn Irwin, my mum, lives forever. Every time you see a sick, injured, orphaned, animal, you'll see Lyn. I love you; I miss you, I long to be reunited with you.'

Few details of Lyn's death emerged at the time, although a death notice in the local paper invited people to attend a gathering at a Sunshine Coast funeral home after a private family service.

Superstars constantly complain about the rumours that surround their lives. Gossip has them getting up to all kinds of mischief and strange business that titillate—affairs, divorces, face lifts, illegitimate children. Inevitably Steve and Terri Irwin became the targets of cruel rumours involving death and separation. In fact rumours of his death, he liked to say whenever they occurred, were greatly exaggerated. 'I get that one all the time,' he said. 'But, as far as I can tell, I'm still here.'

But it became hurtful when the rumours involved his and Terri's marriage. When he heard false reports that his 10-year marriage to Terri was on the rocks he shook his head with a rueful smile. 'People can say what they like, but the fact is that Terri and I are as close as two people could possibly be,' he said, explaining that some people could not handle it when others were happy. 'I was driving down to Brissie (Brisbane) the other day and some radio station was talking about how Terri had gone back to live in the United States and I was meant to be with some new sheila … and I laughed my head off. We've both heard the story and it cracks us up.'

Terri showed her own contempt for the scandal-mongering by turning it into a joke. 'It is not true that Steve and I have split, but it is true that I used to be a man,' she said. 'Look, when you are in the public eye like we are and when you are as popular as Steve is, you expect all kind of rumours to pop up. With the whole "Steve is dead" thing—and believe me, in the States there are stories about his supposed demise every day—we just put a humourous spin on it by putting out a "Steve Lives" surfwear label.'

In July 2006, the tiny Pacific nation of Vanuatu, with a population of 200,000, was declared 'the happiest place on the planet' in a global survey conducted by the New Economics Foundation and Friends of the Earth. The researchers used three factors to identify the winning country—life expectancy, human wellbeing and the damage, or lack of it, caused by the country's 'environmental footprint.'

But on one particular island, Maewo, the villagers had been in a state of happiness for the previous three years, all thanks to Steve Irwin. For he had saved someone from being eaten. At least that's what the islanders, terrified by a 3.6-metre (11-foot) saltwater crocodile that had been prowling their waters, believed. It was thought the crocodile had been washed from the island of Vanua Lava during a cyclone in 1998 to the island of Ambae and from there pushed on to Maewo by further bad weather in 2002. This, said environmentalists who travelled to the area and managed to look at the crocodile through binoculars, was a classic example of a reptile that had been displaced from its territory, shot, injured and had then become a problem.

The villagers of Maewo were terrified of it. Children were afraid to go to the beach; the women were scared to do their washing in the river; the men just refused to have anything to do with it.

I knew their fear. Vanuatu is my wife's homeland and in travels through many of the outer islands with her I learned of the sheer terror that many people had of crocodiles and sharks. The islands were alive with rumours of ghosts and dead people walking and to have to worry about lurking crocodiles and prowling sharks was just too much. So it was understandable that when a large croc seemed to be waiting around for the chance to grab someone, a search began for someone who could get rid of it. The police had a go at shooting it, but succeeded only in injuring it and then someone raised Steve Irwin's name, for his reputation as a Crocodile Hunter had reached even that remote area.

A plea for help was duly sent to the Australia Zoo's International Crocodile Rescue, which Steve had set up. He sent his senior croc experts, Brian Coulter and Toby Millyard to Vanuatu in February 2003 to assess the problem. It was the start of a long and frustrating operation, brought to a successful fruition with Steve's expert involvement and guidance. The crocodile, which had already taken livestock and was posing a threat to humans, was in a dangerous mood, the two men from Steve's zoo concluded, because it had been badly wounded by the Mobile Force whose efforts to kill it had failed. Too terrified to get any closer themselves, they had given up and returned to the capital, Port Vila.

The zoo's advance team rang Steve to work out a game plan. It was decided the best way to catch the crocodile would be to use a floating trap set up in front of the village of Narovorovo, where the reptile was usually to be found. Its latest kill, though had been near the village of Navenevene, 90 minutes walk north of Narovorovo, where it had taken a pig. Finally the team saw it swimming some 200 metres (650 feet) offshore, surfacing every 10 minutes for a five minute interval for air before sinking below again. The trap, set up near Narovorovo, was anchored to a pier. Parts of a chicken were placed near the front of the trap in the hope of luring the crocodile in, but the crocodile ignored the bait. Then heavy winds,the fringe of cyclone Erica 200 kilometres (124 miles) north west of Vanuatu, swept through the islands making the trap unsteady in the rising swell. It was, one of the team reported later, a 'shit of a day'.

The team were lashed by torrential rain and powerful onshore winds. The crocodile was sighted again but now the problem was that the bait had been washed away. There was no way the croc was going to enter the trap without something in it. But it came ashore anyway, riding the swell like a Bondi surfer. The team thought it was exhausted and was allowing itself to be carried around by the tide. At last they were able to get a good look at it and estimated it was some 3.5 metres (11 feet) long. Just then, as Coulter and Millyard cautiously approached, excited villagers ran down to the beach to see the crocodile and it immediately turned and went straight back into the water.

Then disaster struck—the winds and the tide swept the whole trap away. Six days passed and any hope that the trap might be found slipped away. The croc had also disappeared. The team continued to monitor the beach and checked with transport drivers for any word of sightings, but there was none. Storms raged and there was no sign of the lost trap or the crocodile. Finally, after checking with Steve back at the zoo, it was decided the team should return to Australia, build another trap and return to Vanuatu as soon as possible.

Steve, the ultimate expert, listened carefully to his frustrated team's report when they gathered at the zoo. The crocodile, they told him, occupied a large territory—more than 20 kilometres (12 miles)—and trapping him had already proved to be a time-consuming exercise. They still believed a floating trap was the best means of catching him but in any case there seemed little point in returning until after the cyclone season at the end of May. Reinforcements would need to be built into a new trap.

Steve realised the dilemma he and his team faced. There was no way he would contemplate having the animal destroyed, despite its injuries, without further examination. In all event, it was very important to try to keep it alive to maintain the conservation of saltwater crocodiles. Vanuatu is the most easterly point of their range from Australia and, because very few crocodiles are seen on those islands, they were classified as highly endangered in that Pacific region. Yet on the other hand the crocodile posed a threat to the livestock and children on the island of Maewo. It was a dilemma. There was an answer, though, to the current and any future problem that might involve a visiting crocodile: villagers must change their understanding of the creatures and adapt their lifestyles so that any croc is accommodated without posing a direct danger.

In the meantime, something had to be done quickly. Because the villagers were coastal people, their daily routines had been affected by this particular crocodile's presence They could not fish, swim or dive—important aspects of their culture.

'We've just got to get back there and sort all this out,' Steve said after reading through his team's detailed reports.

Brian Coulter returned first in mid–May and began assembling the new trap which he anchored at the mouth of a river. The mouth of the river had been silted up by the high tides and strong currents precipitated by the recent storm. It was because the crocodile's source of fresh water had been cut off that it stayed away from the area. Brian dug away at the barricade at the river mouth to start an easy flow of water again, then hung the carcass of a small pig at the entrance to the newly erected trap.

He then began searching the coast, calling at villages to ask if the crocodile had been seen recently. No, it had not. But as he returned to Norovorovo he learned from a truck driver that the crocodile had been spotted in a remote area near a waterfall north of the village. When Brian reached the area there was no sign of the crocodile.

He devised a new game plan—to have the trap towed up through the ocean at the rear of a small motorboat and placed at the waterfall. He set up a bush camp south of Navenevene, and, with the trap in place and a 15 kilogram pig carcass being used as bait, waited. Every hour, in the lashing rain, he checked the trap. He did not see the reptile but villagers who passed through the area daily said there had been several recent sightings.

It was turning out, once again, to be a frustrating mission, but Brian knew help was at hand—Steve would soon be joining him! Then on 21 May he saw the crocodile some 200 metres (650 feet) from the trap. When he checked the trap six hours later the gate was still up. He waited in the incessant rain until darkness fell and swept the area with his torch: no eyeshine.

Finally, success. A later check of the trap revealed that the crocodile was inside. Knowing that Steve would be arriving the following day, Brian kept watch on the crocodile, which remained placidly inside the trap—until two sharks approached and began circling the cage, attracted by the pig carcass which was floating around inside with the crocodile. When the croc made a threatening display by splashing the water, the sharks took off. There was danger everywhere, for croc and man.

On Steve's arrival the two men began bringing the trap in, cutting the anchor lines and hauling it into the shallows. As a crowd from the village watched, the crocodile's top jaw was roped and then to clapping, cheers and whoops of delight from the crowd, Steve jumped on the crocodile's back and secured its head with tape as Brian helped with his extra weight on the tail area.

Then Steve and his friend set about assessing the crocodile's injuries. It was confirmed he was a male and he had been shot twice—once in the right eye and once in the front left leg. There on the stony beach the crocodile men carried out an operation to remove the bullets, treat the wounds and give the animal antibiotics to assist the healing process. Brian injected the right eye, which had been damaged beyond repair, with long acting penicillin.

The croc was then blindfolded and secured in a specially designed canvas crocodile sock for transportation to the airport. It was loaded onto a charter flight—which had had its seats removed—accompanied by Steve and Brian. Photographs show Steve sitting on the small plane beside what would be the strangest passenger the airline company had ever issued a ticket to—the big croc rolled up in a sack.

The reptile was flown to the island of Vanua Lava, 180 kilometres (111 miles) to the north, where it had originated before the storm swept it away. On arrival at Sola, on Vanua Lava, the crocodile was carried to the clean, fresh waters of the Selva River for release. As Steve and Brian were to report later: 'The release site is a beautiful freshwater river, lined with pandanus and coastal hibiscus, perfect for crocodile habitat, and the crocodile could not wait to get into it.'

The two men were not yet ready to return to the Australia Zoo, however. There was another job to be done. While in Sola they held educational talks on crocodile safety and biology for the fascinated villagers. Then, just before they were due to leave they carried out a quick survey of the region to try to establish how their crocodile was doing. They saw him near the place of release, a shallow tributary, but later, as they flew away from the island, they took one last look and saw their troublesome friend swimming up the Selva River. 'Mission accomplished!' Steve declared.

Of course, the cameras were rolling all the time, and Steve explained why to the people of Vanuatu. In a letter to Mr Russell Nari, Deputy Director of the Environment Unit in the island group, Steve said: 'The successful relocation of the crocodile is the greatest message that we can give to the world about the protection of an endangered species and, through my television program, the whole world will learn how compassionate the people of Vanuatu are in allowing the rescue operation to take place and at the same time showcase the beauty of the islands.'

Steve's name echoed around Vanuatu. Mr Nari, in a public statement, said: 'Our main concern during this whole project has been to maintain the wellbeing of both the local people and the crocodile and with today's successful capture and relocation, everybody has been delighted with the result.'

He thanked a number of officials and chiefs living on the islands, adding his appreciation of the help given by a number of volunteers, but reserved the best to last. He wanted to give his thanks 'above all' to 'Steve Irwin and the team from the Australia Zoo for a great partnership in the rescue.'

In the towns and villages of Vanuatu people who had not heard of Steve Irwin the Crocodile Hunter wanted to know more about him. They wanted to know when he was coming back. Rumour had it that he had bought land in Vanuatu for conservation purposes. But this was not so.

However, he was buying land in Australia every time cash came in from zoo takings, his movie, the television documentaries and whenever suitable areas of wilderness became available. An acquisition in 2003 was a property between Roma and St George in Queensland, taking his total holding to 26,000 hectares. He was working at preserving the Brigalow belt, one of the most endangered habitats in Australia, containing some of the rarest and highly endangered species, including the northern hairy-nosed wombat, the stripe-faced dunnart and the eastern star finch.

'Each time we get payments, we put it straight into conservation work,' Steve said, pointing out he had also bought a piece of very denuded land in an area known as Crows Nest, where koalas lived. Extremely endangered, the marsupial population had grown from about 10 to 30 following the planting of 50,000 gum trees.

Whenever Steve Irwin took up the challenge, the creatures of the wild benefited.

9

Baby Bob Meets a Croc

To hear people say that it was a publicity stunt, that I'm just like Michael Jackson, well, it just tears me up. It makes me sick to my stomach to be compared in that way.

In the eyes of most viewers of his documentaries Steve could do no wrong. He was mobbed every time he appeared somewhere in the flesh. Overseas he epitomised what many perceived as the stereotype Australian, inadvertently helping to preserve the image some Britons had of kangaroos hopping down the main streets of the big cities, where everyone wore hats with corks dangling from them.

He was a mega-star. The multimillion-dollar selling of Steve Irwin included everything from action figures of him and his wife, along with a number of toothy toy crocs to even a pinball machine portraying his image. There was, too, a character based on Steve who appeared in an episode of *South Park*.

Curiously—or perhaps understandably—his antics did not wear so well with his fellow Australians, many of whom applauded his work among wildlife but rejected the clowning that went along with it.

'At best,' commented Sydney writer Michael Idato, 'he was a jolly Queensland curiosity … at worst, he was an ocker-sounding self-parody …' He added that Steve's popularity abroad, which long ago eclipsed that of Paul Hogan's Crocodile Dundee, served as 'a powerful lesson in the changing nature of modern celebrity and the immense power of television as a platform for such fame.'

Towards the end of 2003, Terri was preparing for an important event. Pregnant with their second child, she was expecting its arrival in December. If it was a boy, said Steve with a twinkle in his eye, he wouldn't mind calling him 'Bluey', although he admitted that Terri wouldn't have a bar of that. But first he had another assignment to fulfil—and it turned out to be far more dramatic than he could have ever imagined. For Steve became a real-life action hero, saving an injured diver off the coast of Mexico in early November.

As he and the television crew were filming sea lions and hammer-head sharks in the Sea of Cortez, off Mexico's long strip of land known as the Baja Peninsula, they heard from other boats in the area that two American divers had been missing for more than two hours.

Steve immediately ordered filming to stop so that his boat could be used to help in the search. He then used his satellite phone to call in a search plane. He realised that time was of the essence, for one diver, Katie Vrooman was 77 years old and her friend, Scott Jones was in his 60s. The seas were becoming rough and fears were held for both. With a search party and a plane organised, Steve spent most of the day and late into the night looking for the couple, without success. He reluctantly stopped for a few hours sleep but resumed at first thing the following morning.

'We weren't going to give up,' Steve said when he recalled the drama. 'Then two kayakers came out to us and said they had spotted a bloke on the rocks.' Steve launched a dinghy and he and two other men raced to a small island. Submerged rocks made it impossible to get the dinghy in close right away. They could see a man, who was obviously Jones, clinging on to the rocks for dear life and it looked like he might be lost at any moment.

Not wanting to waste another second, Steve ignored his own safety and dived in. He swam the last 300 metres through what seemed like impossible seas. Clambering up the rocks, Steve hung onto the exhausted man until the dinghy could be brought in close.

Steve helped Jones aboard before taking him back to the larger craft where he was given food and water. There was no sign of Miss Vrooman. It was established later that she had drowned—a tragedy that Jones had already relayed to Steve. The rescued man told the Australian that they got into trouble in the rough waters and then the strong current swept her towards some rocks which she hit. Jones had managed to reach her and tried to revive her.

He clung on to her on the rocks for several hours as waves pounded him and then, when exhaustion set in, Miss Vrooman slipped from his grasp.

'What he went through … I mean, I just happened to be there with the right resources at hand,' said Steve, brushing aside suggestions he had been the hero of the day. 'Scott, he held on to his mate all night and he wasn't going to let her go, no matter what. He's the hero of this story, not me.'

Steve headed home to Terri to be with her for the birth of their next child. But first there was some business to complete. Negotiations were concluded for him to receive a $A175,000 fee for appearing in a Federal Government quarantine awareness television campaign in which he warned people to be careful about bringing insects into the country from abroad. The money, he declared, would not go into his pocket but would go into the non-profit Steve Irwin Wildlife Fund. It would also go towards completing, staffing and running a new koala hospital which he expected to open six months later.

At the end of November 2003, Steve and Terri knew that the birth of their next child was imminent. Looking at Terri's swollen figure he was reminded of the time a heavily pregnant woman who had turned up at a shopping centre to attend a screening of his crocodile movie had asked him to autograph her belly. Ever the entertainer, Steve grabbed a pen and, staring at the exposed tummy declared: 'Crikey! That's a real beauty you've got there!' After writing his name he added something special—a drawing of a crocodile.

They celebrated the birth of baby Robert Clarence Irwin—to be known from henceforth as Bob—on 1 December, 2003. Steve remembered the publicity he had received when he introduced Bindi to the boa constrictor, for after he had first put reptile and baby together for my camera, there were many other instances when he repeated the performance.

The child was never in any danger, he would tell onlookers, for the snake was well and truly always wrapped around his neck and if it had opened its mouth he would have had Bindi out of harm's way in a flash.

He may have felt he could not repeat the 'snake and baby show' with Bob because people might remark they had seen it all before. What he needed was something different—and when he came up with an idea it was certainly different—and more. It was explosive. On 2 January, 2004, he took baby Bob into the pen where Murray the crocodile lived and holding the baby aloft told a live audience through a small microphone he was wearing: 'He's one month old, so it's about time Bob did his first croc demo.'

He then proceeded to dangle a chicken carcass over the four metre crocodile's gaping jaws—once the reptile had emerged from its pool—while holding Bob in his arms. The crowd 'oo-ed and ah'ed' as the crocodile reared up to take the meat, snatching it in its jaws and consuming it in a second. 'Good boy, Bob,' said Steve.

Terri looked on as her husband then 'walked' Bob along the ground, holding him by his arms, towards the crocodile pool as Murray lurked close by.

Cameras snapped away. Video cameras whirred. Pictures of that astonishing scene found their way to Australia's newspapers and the television news. Then they shot around the world. It was major news everywhere, not because of any wildlife message but because Steve was suddenly under attack for what was seen at the very least as child abuse; at worst, putting the baby's life in danger. The switchboards of two Australian television stations that broadcast the incident were jammed with complaints. Newspaper switchboards could hardly keep up with the flood of angry callers.

The pictures and story had become a major talking point—and most of it was unkind. The Crocodile Hunter, in the eyes of the world, had made a huge mistake. The incident was likened to Michael Jackson's moment of madness when he dangled his baby son out of a hotel window in Germany in 2002.

Steve's actions provoked an immediate response from the Australian Family Association, which joined other groups in saying that his behaviour was tantamount to child abuse. 'Most parents would cringe at the sight of such things,' said Bill Muehlenberg, a spokesman for the family association. 'One slip, one fall and he [the baby] is the crocodile's lunch.'

London's *Daily Mirror* ran the story on its front page under the heading: 'Crocky Horror Show'. Another paper ran the heading: 'Steve Irwin—Australian for Stupid'. In America, the *New York Post* headline read: 'Crocodile Shock. Irwin's Sick Baby Stunt', then asked 'Has Steve Irwin gone off his croc-er?' The *New York Daily News* said he managed to 'one-up Jackson in the child care department', then gave its own definition of Australian for good parenting: 'Taunting a 13ft crocodile with your infant son'. Joining in the frenzy was the

San Diego Union-Tribune, which ran slides of the incident on its website along with a description: 'Steve Irwin holds tyke, feeds croc.'

If Steve had been expecting support from television audiences who loved his crocodile hunting shows, he would not have been encouraged by the enormous exposure the networks gave to the incident. CNN ran a website poll asking people if they thought Steve had 'endangered his baby'. Of 12,000 votes that flooded in, 61 per cent said he had. Even Animal Planet, the cable channel that broadcasts *The Crocodile Hunter* in America, announced that it did not support any activity that intentionally put a child 'in harm's way'.

In an official statement that would have both saddened and—to some extent—heartened Steve, the channel said: 'Based on the footage we have seen, we believe a mistake was made. That said, we know from the many years we have worked with Steve, that his family is the most important thing in his life.'

The statement did little to placate Animal Planet fans. On the channel's Internet discussion board they unleashed their anger. One said: 'I admire your work very much, Steve, but I think you took it too macho this time. Exposing that innocent baby to danger does not make him more brave or you more smart in the eyes of the public.'

Closer to home, Keith Cook, owner of a crocodile farm near Cairns, in northern Queensland, could not believe what he had seen on his television. He described Steve as a Hollywood version of Daniel Boone, adding: 'I think he's a bloody idiot—he's addicted to the attention.'

At the Australia Zoo, Steve held a press conference, his wife at his side as microphones were thrust forward and cameras focused on his concerned face, for this was not something he was used to—defending his actions. Baby Bob, he insisted was never in any danger. Later, as the heat increased and more demands came in from around the world for interviews, Steve's publicist John Harrison said he had taken a short holiday to consider everything.

Not surprisingly, Steve had his supporters, who flooded Internet websites to say they had not been shocked. 'I don't see a problem with this,' said one writer. 'The baby would be in more danger if its father was drunk … Steve knew exactly what he was doing and wouldn't let a shred of harm come to his child.'

Another comment supported the view that Steve was in full control: 'There was about 10 fellas waiting just out of the picture if something was to go wrong.'

'As he said,' remarked another writer, 'his parents did exactly the same thing, and he did the same thing with Bindy. It's sort of like their family tradition.'

From the Australian Reptile Park at Gosford, in NSW, came words of support from owner John Weigel, a friend of Steve's. The crocodile, he said, had no chance of reaching the baby, adding: 'If that was a lion, it could run forward and capture the child but the reality of a 12-foot crocodile with tiny legs and enormous mass … it doesn't happen.'

A widely acknowledged crocodile expert, Grahame Webb, professor of wildlife management at the Charles Darwin University, said that while he was critical of Steve's actions it was doubtful that Murray could have jumped and grabbed the baby from the position it was in. The real danger, he said, would have come if Steve had slipped or fell.

Steve, in fact, had not gone far for his short holiday as stated by his publicist. A few days later he appeared on Australia's Channel Nine's *A Current Affair* and was unrepentant. He would do it again, he said, but with a difference—'I would make sure there were no cameras around.' He added: 'I will continue to educate my children and the children of the world so they don't go into the water with crocs.'

As a public relations exercise, he admitted the feeding show with baby Bob had been a disaster, but he didn't care about his reputation. 'You know what? Take everything away from me ... take my zoo, take my life, take the croc, I don't care. The most important thing I have got in my life is my kids. That's it. My family, mate.'

For the viewers he reflected on the time when his father Bob had taken him into a crocodile pen when he was just a baby and Steve said he felt the need to educate his children in a similar way. 'In fact, when I was nine years old, he let me capture my first crocodile. You would make sure that your kids went into this world understanding the dangers of their surroundings. Mate, if you were in my boots, you'd do the same thing.'

He wanted to make the point that a tape from an Australia Zoo camera, shooting the incident from a different angle, would help to clear his name. 'All that ugly, stacked-up vision of me looking like I endangered my child will be put to bed very quickly,' he insisted.

Despite the raging controversy, the Queensland Government continued to stand by its decision to nominate Steve as the Australian of the Year for all that he had done for wildlife, the environment and the country's tourism industry. He retained odds of 4-1 with a betting agency to win the Australian of the Year title, lying second behind retiring Australian cricket captain Steve Waugh.

Terri told the world that she had not been worried when Steve took Bob into the crocodile's enclosure. 'It was a wonderful sensory experience for Bob,' she said. 'He dug it.'

The incident would not go away. Television shows repeated the footage time and again. Steve told one interviewer that Bob was quite safe and he would have only fallen over with the child in his arms if a meteor had hit the earth and caused an earthquake of 6.6 on the Richter scale. Steve, supported by Terri, had put up a brave, if not defiant, front in the face of international criticism, but away from the microphones and cameras he was deeply hurt.

It did not help matters when, the day after the Baby Bob incident, Terri stunned zoo visitors when she reportedly referred to daughter Bindi, then aged five, as 'white meat' during a live show. Bindi had reportedly been told by her parents to enter a new enclosure adjoining a crocodile pen and then splash around to encourage the reptiles to swim out. There was a closed gate between the pool and the pen. Then, as Bindi splashed the water, Terri is said to have called out: 'Now flail around and look helpless. That's the girl, good girl. That's my girl Bindi Irwin, the other white meat.'

Queensland's *Sunday Mail* managed to beat all the competition shortly afterwards with an exclusive interview that saw Steve opening up his heart. He wept as he told the paper that he was even considering withdrawing from public life following accusations that he was a bad father. The worldwide attack had left him and his family 'absolutely devastated'.

Denying he was an irresponsible parent, he said he had simply been carrying on a family tradition started by his father. 'I am not a bad parent. I am not an irresponsible parent. I am not a bad father,' he said. 'If you knew how much I loved my kids—well, any parent can tell you about the love they feel for their children—but if you knew how much I love them, then you would know that I would never, ever, put them in any danger. Not in a million years. I would lay down my life for Bindi and Bob.'

Referring to the Baby Bob show, he said: 'To hear people say that it was a publicity stunt, that I'm just like Michael Jackson dangling his baby over a balcony, well it just tears me up inside.' His was not a normal family living with a normal backyard. 'You have to understand the sort of upbringing I had, the sort of upbringing my kids are going to have.'

Steve questioned whether it had been a good idea to open up his family life to the world. He said it was 'fair enough' that he had done that, but it was to spread the word about wildlife, about his family's passion for wildlife. 'Now I'm really questioning if that's the right way to go.' The criticism had hit his own father badly, he revealed. Father Bob, who had been away, was driving to the zoo when he heard the outrage that followed the incident and had to pull over to the side of the road, too distressed to continue driving. 'I just spoke to him and he was just crying and crying by the truck,' said Steve.

Later, when he appeared on Andrew Denton's show *Enough Rope* he was given the chance of putting his side of the story forward once more. He showed camera angles that he said revealed that he and the baby were further away from the crocodile than had originally looked.

'Baby Bob is in my left arm, nowhere near the croc. Mate, I've got orang-outang arms and so that is the safest thing with wildlife you ever do. That, that is in essence what I've done with my daughter Bindi, because you've got to teach kids about wildlife when they're tiny. I start, I started like when they're in the womb, because they're soaking up information, they're soaking up sounds and smells inside the womb, so when they're very young, they have to learn crocs right then. Because if you leave it till they get to two, three, five years of age, they're scared, they have nightmares, they panic and they are out of control … you can't do wildlife like that.'

Denton pointed out that when babies are one month old, as Bob was, they can't distinguish their dad's face. Their brains were still in a formative stage. 'Is he really going to learn about a croc when his brain is still that basic?'

Steve replied: 'Absolutely' before saying that people should see his daughter Bindi, 'the most well-rounded, croc-savvy child on the face of the earth'. He said that if his children weren't croc-savvy, then he was a bad parent. But Bindi was good testimony to his and Terri's parenting.

Terri wanted to have her say about the incident and the ongoing upbringing of baby Bob. 'It's not like we were teaching Robert how to hand feed a crocodile. You know, we're not like teaching him "Okay Robert, go get him". It's just simply the way you share time with any child.'

Denton had more to ask about the incident, drawing Steve's attention to criticism that he had not supported the baby's neck as he walked him towards the pool. The television host said: 'I think the thing that I know a lot of people said to me at the time was, the thing that really bothered them, was when you were walking Bob, they were worried about the neck support. When you look back at that now, do you think, "Mmm, I don't think I did that quite right?"'

Steve would hear nothing of it. 'Not at all, no, not at all,' he replied. 'No, he's a, he's a strong little bugger, mate. He, he's you know he's very strong. No, no, I don't think the neck thing … you know I've never really thought about it.' He then asked Terri to continuing discussing it with Denton because he personally didn't think there was a problem. She made it clear that she saw nothing wrong in what Steve had done.

'Traditionally dads don't touch babies,' she said. 'They don't have anything to do with them and it's cotton wool and all this kind of stuff and it would be really nice if dads would actually pick up babies and know the head just doesn't lob off—it doesn't. And in fact at no time did Robert's head tilt. It was always up, it was always up, he never tilted.'

Steve admitted he was totally surprised by the reaction—'totally broadsided' was the way he described it. They were having a big family day 'and then bang, we just got struck a devastating blow. You know, we've got a bead on it now, but you know we're forging ahead and really sorry that we scared anyone, but you know we are kind of like the Addams family. We don't live a normal life.'

So it continued along the vein of Steve and Terri defending the Baby Bob show and insisting that it was something very normal for them as a family. Steve summed it up by saying that he did not lead a normal lifestyle. He lived in the middle of a zoo with a hundred crocodiles surrounding him and venomous snakes in the back yard. It was a pretty different sort of a place to grow up in and he wanted to raise his children the same as his parents raised him. 'I think that's the secret to good parenting—use techniques that you know work.'

Steve did not get the Australian of the Year award for 2003. It went instead to epidemiologist Professor Fiona Stanley, followed the next year by former Australian cricket captain Steve Waugh who had been captain since 1999.

11

Victims and Heroes in Croc Territory

I have no fear of losing my life. If I have to save a koala or a crocodile or a kangaroo or a snake, mate, I will save it.

No-one needed to read between the lines as they listened to Steve and Terri's defence of the incident to be aware that they had been deeply shocked by the worldwide reaction to the Baby Bob incident. But if they didn't know it before, one other factor stood out—that the couple were deeply in love and very supportive of one another. It was Steve, of course, who was on the receiving end of the attacks but Terri was not going to let him stand in the public spotlight and take it on his own. She was going to remain at his side and fend off the arrows with him.

'Terri's very calming,' he said of her. 'She's really quite stable. She's like a big chunk of concrete, very solid very stable, very neutral, very "Switzerland".'

Like Steve, she'd grown up close to her parents, Clarence and Judy, learning all about her father's construction business from a young age. It was Clarence who taught her how to type when she

RICHARD SHEARS

148

was eight, while her mother made sure her spelling was correct. As she was to recall, she didn't play with dolls; instead, while still at school, she set up a business, selling everything from old toys to bottles of juice. One of her proudest photographs shows her as a young girl sitting at an outdoor table waiting for customers to come along and sample the juice she had poured into a big jug. Then, of course, she had gone on to set up her Cougar Country rehabilitation centre, with her family supporting her all the way.

So Terri was as much a family girl as Steve was a family boy. When they came together they formed a strong bond. Steve was to need this, for if he thought controversy had finally left him, there was more to come. Several months after the Baby Bob affair there was further uproar when Steve was accused of upsetting wildlife in Antarctica by getting too close to a pod of whales and even sliding down the snowy slopes with a group of penguins, his arms flailing.

It was claimed he had broken both international and Australian federal laws by getting so close to the creatures. Of course, the cameras were on him at all times and the crew were convinced they had some very marketable material. Such was the outrage in the wake of the baby and the croc incident that Steve's critics were convinced that, having escaped any form of punishment the first time around, he would face charges for his Antarctic escapades. The maximum fine for interacting with Antarctic wildlife was $A1 million and two years in jail.

After the Australian Environment Department viewed footage provided by the Irwins, however, Prime Minister John Howard announced that, following a month-long investigation, no charges would be laid.

'I've been told that after a proper examination, a decision has been taken that no action of any kind is necessary,' said Mr Howard.

However, there were claims from some quarters that the real story of what happened down there in the snowy wastelands had been edited out of the footage. In time, Steve and Terri released their version of the incidents in a special Crocodile Hunter documentary entitled *Crocodiles and Controversy*. But there was no doubt he had been hurt and he was deeply grateful to those of his friends and fellow Australians in general who had stood by him through the Baby Bob and the Antarctic controversies.

'Crikey, I am very proud to be an Australian son,' he told Queensland's *Sunday Mail,* 'because when the chips are down you can always count on your mates to put out their hand. I want to assure everyone that I would never do anything to harm our precious wildlife whatsoever; that I just want to get animals into people's hearts and promote the conservation of our rapidly diminishing native animals.'

Among his staunchest supporters was the Queensland Premier, Peter Beattie, who had not only continued to support Steve's nomination for the Australian of the Year Award, but had told the Crocodile Hunter's critics to 'call the dogs off'. He added: 'Steve is a showman and can be outrageous but he doesn't deserve this.' His critics, said Mr Beattie, would do better to turn their attention to the whaling countries of Japan, Iceland and Norway.

'I have known Steve since I first started in television,' said wildlife ranger Stacey Thomson, a familiar voice on Queensland radio and a well-known face on television's *Totally Wild*. 'Australia Zoo was just a small animal park and I think he is a good ambassador for Queensland. In his mind he really wants to support the conservation cause. He does it in a way that some people don't like, but I am a big fan and a big supporter.'

Messages of support continued to pour into the zoo. Tourism Queensland boss Terry Jackman described Steve as 'the Paul Hogan of this generation' but Steve's friends said he was much bigger than Hogan or his movie character Crocodile Dundee.

Controversy continued to dog Steve in another area—his fight to prevent crocodiles being killed in the Northern Territory.

True to his beliefs, he was totally against a plan by the Northern Territory Government and crocodile expert Grahame Webb to allow a number of saltwater crocs to be culled each year. Their numbers have grown to around 70,000 in the territory—a huge jump from the dwindling population of less than 5000 recorded in the late 1940s as a result of hunting. In the early 1970s, a ban was imposed on hunting them and exporting their skins and their numbers began to recover. Professor Webb, who led the program to build up the numbers, wanted landowners to see them as an economic asset and not as pests and he was working with the territory government on a scheme that would give them commercial value.

Under a strict quota system, landholders were given the chance to harvest and sell crocodiles and their eggs each year. Professor Webb said it was in the interests of landholders to open suitable farms on their own land while others could be maintained on Aboriginal reserves. The scheme moved along successfully, with some 20,000 eggs being sold each year for $A40 each, while 600 crocodiles were harvested for around $A500 each. What Professor Webb wanted further was a program that would include big game hunters from America and Europe, who would pay $A10,000 for the chance to hunt down and shoot a single crocodile. He and the Northern Territory government realised that the hunters would want to take the head and skins of their catches back home with them and approaches were made to the Federal Government for approval to export 25 skins of crocodiles hunted on safari.

This is where Steve has stepped in. On his advice and after strong campaigning, Federal Environment Minister Ian Campbell has repeatedly turned down the request to allow crocodile safaris. 'There's only one way to shoot a crocodile,' Steve told the minister. 'And that's with a camera.'

But Professor Webb said he could not understand Steve's argument, which he said was 'absurd when you have animals eating people'. The real goal of people like him and other activists, said Professor Webb, was to 'have all of us just eating vegetables'. He asked: 'How would Melbourne or Sydney people go with crocodiles in their backyards? I can tell you, they would lose their patience very quickly.'

Speaking to Lindsay Murdoch, Northern Territory correspondent for *The Age* newspaper, Professor Webb added: 'Nothing is to be gained from being cruel to animals. But our conservation program up here is at stake because landowners have to have an incentive to put up with crocodiles—it's important that landowners see them as an asset.'

Crocodiles would kill even more people in northern Australia, he said, but for a strong education program. 'The reality is that these things can kill you and we have done a remarkably good job living with them.'

Despite what may be regarded as large numbers of crocodiles, Steve has pointed out that the 'salties' are categorised as vulnerable, which is one step away from endangered. The east coast of Queensland in particular, he had established, still contained low densities of crocodiles and it was vital to maintain a healthy population. But one of the problems, in the wake of a number of attacks on humans, had been fear.

Inevitably, with each fatality over the years there have been calls for crocodiles to be culled, although in fairness many people have accepted that the main problem has always been humans encroaching on crocodile territory.

I have written numerous stories about attacks where, in many cases, it has been human error that has brought about a fatality. The biggest error has been ignorance—people have died because they have failed to recognise they are in crocodile territory and need to exercise great care, or, worse, they have totally ignored warning signs not to camp, swim or wash their cars in a river. The signs are self explanatory in any language, depicting a picture of a swimmer with a 'banned' emblem across the image, while underneath is the head of a crocodile.

Detailed instructions are also displayed in places urging campers to stay away from the water's edge whether taking a stroll or fishing in areas where crocodiles are known to exist. People are warned not to return to exactly the same place each day because a crocodile will remember those habits and lie in wait.

Fishermen are urged not to clean fish near the water or throw in scraps. Pieces of food should not be left lying around camp sites. When launching a boat, everyone should avoid going into the water and no-one should dangle arms or legs over the side. As for boats, any flimsy craft, particularly one that might sink if it hits an obstruction or overturn easily, should be left on shore.

In recent years there have several fatalities that could have been avoided. In one inexcusable case, it was a tour guide's negligence that led to the death of a young German backpacker, Isabel von Jordon, who drowned in a billabong in the Kakadu National Park in October 2002. She had been invited to go for a swim at night in the still waters by her tour guide, Glenn Robless. The night air was filled with Miss von Jordon's screams as a 4.6-metre (15-foot) crocodile grabbed her, puncturing her left lung and fracturing ribs, before dragging her under and drowning her. The coroner found the guide's invitation to Miss Jordon to go for a swim in the waterhole to be 'inexplicable, indefensible and grossly negligent'.

A year after that tragedy came a terrifying incident, again brought on by a flouting of the rules.

Three young men from the Darwin area had been riding their four-wheeled quad bikes through the bush when they stopped by the fast-flowing Finniss River to wash the mud off their machines. Suddenly, as 22-year-old Brett Mann was standing waist-deep in the fast-flowing river, swollen by recent heavy rains, he lost his footing and began to be carried away. He managed to grab a branch and his two friends, Shaun Blowers and Ashley McGough, both 19, swam after him to help him back. Just as they started to work their way back to the river bank, a 4-metre (13-foot) saltwater crocodile grabbed Brett and pulled him under.

Shocked and terrified, Shaun and Ashley swam to the nearest, partially submerged tree and scrambled up. Two minutes later the crocodile brought Brett's body to the surface and, as Shaun put it 'pretty much showed him off to us and off he swam'.

The young men's terror increased when the crocodile returned to stalk the tree. So there the friends remained right through the night, with the crocodile waiting below. Finally the next day, when their family and friends reported them missing, police found them still clinging to the branches and arranged for them to be winched to safety by helicopter.

I travelled to the Northern Territory to join the police hunt for the crocodile that had taken Brett. One officer, armed with a rifle, explained to me as we stood on the banks of the Finniss that they wanted to track down the crocodile because it might kill again but it was also necessary to find Brett's body so that his family could have closure. It meant shooting any crocodile suspected of being the attacker and cutting it open to look for human remains.

As it transpired, several crocodiles were shot—but no remains were found.

RICHARD SHEARS

September 2005 saw two fatal attacks in less than a week in the Northern Territory. The body of British mines supervisor Russell Harris, 37, from Eastwood, near Nottingham, was found in a river on Groote Eylandt Island a day after he disappeared while snorkelling with a friend off Picnic Beach on 24 September. Although none of his friends had seen a crocodile earlier, Northern Territory police said his injuries indicated that one of the reptiles known to habit the rivers was responsible. Later police said a 4-metre (13-foot) crocodile had been spotted in the area.

Six days after that attack, a Darwin man, Russell Butel, 55, was grabbed by a 5-metre (16-foot) saltwater crocodile while diving with a friend some 190 kilometres (120 miles) north east of the city. Mr Butel frequently dived in the area to collect fish for aquariums. When Mr Butel's body was found later police agreed his injuries were consistent with a crocodile attack.

In August, 2005, 60-year-old fisherman Barry Jeffries broke the rules when he went fishing on one of Steve's favourite croc-hunting locations, the Normanby River, putting out onto the water in a flimsy canoe with his wife, Glenda. A large crocodile was attracted to the vessel as Mr Jeffries reeled in a baited fishing line. As it snapped at the bait close to the canoe, Mr Jefferies lunged at the crocodile with an oar, but the reptile grabbed him and pulled him into the water. His wife swam for her life to the shore but nothing could be done to save her husband.

A local tour operator, Tom Rosse, said he was 'flabbergasted' that the couple had ventured onto the water in a canoe past warning signs, adding: 'People have fished that river quite often but they're usually in a 14-foot dinghy—much wider, much more stable and more imposing for the crocodiles.'

As recently as July 2006, an eight-year-old girl was killed by a crocodile while fishing with her family on the Blythe River in remote Arnhem Land, her name withheld by authorities out of respect for Aboriginal beliefs. Residents of the remote Maningrida community went into mourning for the child. 'They all started wailing just before midnight, which means someone had died,' said a resident.

That same river was the scene of a dramatic, but not fatal, attack in November 2003 when Manuel Gandigorrtij was grabbed by a crocodile while washing his hands there. It snapped its jaws onto his leg and he believed he would have died but for the swift actions of his aunt, Margaret Rinybuma, who punched the crocodile on the nose and kicked it, allowing him to break free.

In the face of such danger, humans have shown great courage, none more so than 61-year-old grandmother Alicia Sorohan who, Steve Irwin style, jumped onto a 4.2-metre (13-foot) crocodile's back in 2004 to save one of her fellow campers in the far north of Queensland. At 4am she woke to hear screams for help, only to witness the extraordinary sight of the large crocodile trying to pull her son-in-law, 34-year-old Andrew Kerr, from his tent.

Without a moment's hesitation she jumped onto the crocodile's back and began wrestling with it. It let Mr Kerr go, but it now had Mrs Sorohan by the arm and she might have received fatal injuries had her son Jason not come to the rescue with a gun and shot the reptile. Mrs Sorohan ended up with a broken nose and had to have two metal plates and 12 screws put into her arm. She received Australia's Star of Courage, which recognises citizens for acts of outstanding bravery.

A year later, while still recovering from her injuries, she met Steve at another awards ceremony and joked she would be willing to be his sidekick if he needed one.

'You would think that after the ordeal she's been through that she would be very, very wary and have a stand-off approach to crocodiles,' he said. 'But she's not; she's the exact opposite. She's intrigued by them. My whole family loves her.'

Steve Irwin has always been ready to emphasise that on average, despite the blazing publicity given to each incident, only one person a year is killed by a crocodile, compared to three dying from bee stings—'not to mention, mate, all the car fatalities and the deaths associated with smoking.' 'Croc attacks', he said, 'were almost always the result of wrong behaviour by the victim.'

As his popularity reached megastar heights through the *Crocodile Hunter* television series in America and frequent publicity in Australia, crowds flooded to the Australia Zoo. In 2000, there were more than 200,000 visitors—many of them tourists from America where his shows were a 'must watch'—and a year later the numbers had swelled to 350,000. Twelve months on and an incredible 600,000 tickets were sold and at the time of his death the number had swelled again to 850,000 visitors a year, adults paying $A43 and children $A29.

The zoo managed to topple visitors to the Gold Coast's popular Dreamworld and Sea World entertainment centres to take out the Queensland Tourism industry's major award for the best tourism attraction. As visitor numbers swelled, so did the zoo, with Steve purchasing a further 70 hectares of land around the premises with plans for its expansion.

Among the new projects was the Australian Wildlife Hospital, established in 2004 in a big old avocado packing shed a short distance away. By 2006 it was treating more than 5000 injured native animals a year, whether they were frogs with broken legs or koalas injured by dogs and cats. Steve's enthusiasm for the project was witnessed by none other than the founder of Planet Ark, Jon Dee, who was being given a guided tour of the hospital when a koala that had been hit by a car was brought in. Steve left his important guest standing as he hurried over to the injured animal to check it over.

'What was amazing was seeing Steve who, one minute was being so dynamic and enthusiastic, talking about how he wanted to make his hospital bigger, and then, when they brought this koala in, he was suddenly, so gentle and so concerned,' Jon recalled.

So successful has the zoo been that redevelopment work to provide two operating theatres, treatment rooms and intensive care units, was due to continue late in 2006 thanks to $A2.5 million in federal funding, although a further $A2 million would still be needed.

'Making it bigger and better than Steve dreamed will be our gift to him,' said Gail Gipp, the hospital manager.

The money he was earning from his television deals continued to be poured into the zoo and its animals, with Steve and his wife agreeing they would continue to live in the same modest home in the middle of the zoo grounds. Other funds would be used to purchase those animals which Steve did not catch personally or willingly take in if they were injured or orphaned.

A Queensland tourism source told the Australian Financial Review in 2006: 'In the past five years Steve's park just exploded and went through the roof. He was on a planet all of his own at Australia Zoo. He was such a legend that most visitors went to see Steve, not the animals.'

Among the many foreign visitors who called at the zoo was an Arabian sheik, who turned up with his translator and a number of aides, telling Steve he was ready to donate funds to conservation in Australia. Uncertain how to greet a fully robed sheik, Steve bowed and called him 'Your Majesty'.

Recounting the story, John Stainton said the visitor then asked if Steve would show him 'the camels'. It so happened that the two camels at the zoo were among Steve's most prized animal friends so it was a proud Crocodile Hunter who led the sheik and his entourage to the pen where the camels lived.

'I want to buy them,' the sheik said through his translator. Steve was horrified. There was no way he was going to part with the camels, but the sheik was insisting. Tense moments followed—until the sheik burst out laughing. So did the members of his entourage. For they weren't visiting Arabs at all but a team of actors that John had hired for a wonderful practical joke to pay Steve back for all the jokes he had played on John. 'He never forgave me,' said John. 'He never stopped trying to get me back for that.'

The sheik affair was reminiscent of other robed visitors to the zoo, the first time being when Steve was young and a Tibetan monk was chatting to his father. Turning to gaze at Steve, the monk referred to the boy as young 'Irwin Yogi'.

'I was really angry with him,' Steve said. 'I didn't understand because I was just a kid flat out being eight years old.' He was not happy at all that he'd been called a cartoon character. Many years later a group of Tibetan monks called at the zoo to bless it and the Irwin family. 'And they called me Yogi, too,' said Steve. 'I thought "Here we go, second time around. What is Yogi?"' He found out later they weren't calling him a bear, but revered him as a person with a higher realisation, in his case a unique understanding of wildlife.

There were some animals that Steve and Terri could not bring back with them from their adventures, for there were times when they travelled overseas to film torrid tales of confrontations with other killers. In Africa, Steve put himself face to face with deadly creatures like the black mamba and the Egyptian cobra. In America, Steve met the venomous sidewinder, also known as the horned rattlesnake.

There was no corner of the world that the Irwins were not prepared to travel to in pursuit of good footage. In the highlands of Papua New Guinea, bow-and-arrow tribes who had rarely seen white people, stared in astonishment as the fast-talking Australian threw himself into waterholes to wrestle crocodiles that terrified them. On that same adventure, Steve and Terri mingled with bats, were thrilled at the sight of a rare tree kangaroo and rescued three juvenile orang-outangs. The commentary was never scripted—John Stainton was happy to let Steve talk away, for his natural enthusiasm was far more enthralling than any choreographed draft.

Eventually as their young family started to grow and every inch of the zoo was required for the animals, the couple moved out of their modest home in the grounds and bought a waterfront home at Minyama on the Sunshine Coast, reportedly taking out a mortgage with the ANZ bank. 'No-one's going to deny them that,' said a friend. 'They'd earned the comfort after running around the bush and sleeping in the most awful conditions for so many years.'

Steve's expansion plans for the zoo and the build-up of its attractions did not please everyone. Residents living in the zoo's vicinity were perturbed by his plans to start sightseeing helicopter flights around the Glasshouse Mountains in partnership with the Gubbi Gubbi Aboriginal people. The volcanic range has deep spiritual significance for indigenous people, but the locals said the educational flights would shatter their peaceful lifestyle and go against all that Steve stood for—for the noise from the helicopter would upset wildlife.

'Our main concern revolves around the fact that a helicopter will be flying overhead at the rate of six flights per hour. That's 48 flights a day and it's just not appropriate for this area,' an organiser of a protest, Mr John Weeks, told the *Sunday Mail* newspaper. 'We have not fought with Steve Irwin about his zoo at all. Most people respect Steve for what he has achieved. And if he is going to establish a cultural centre for indigenous people at the zoo, that's a good thing. But we feel he is using the indigenous people and their culture to promote scenic flights.'

There were objections from Aboriginal people too. Mr Ken Murphy, a spokesman for the Jinabarra people, said he was concerned that the zoo had only contacted the Gubbi Gubbi people, even though there were several other native title claimants in the area. 'It's a very significant place to Aboriginal people,' he said. 'It's like flying a helicopter around a church,' he added, claiming, too, that animal and bird life would be frightened by the helicopter.

The zoo, meanwhile, said the helicopter it planned to use in the unrestricted air space—which meant that permission was not required to operate flights in the area—was the quietest and most reliable on the market and the service would also incorporate wildlife rescue, fire fighting and marine animal rescue. It would also be on call for traffic accidents and other emergencies.

As the zoo expanded its facilities, Steve and Terri agreed that while it was important to maintain a high television profile if their message was to get across, it was equally important that visitors to the zoo could get close to the animals they had come to see—it was all part of the learning process. Callers today can physically touch and cuddle wombats, non-venomous snakes, lizards, tortoises, dingoes wombats and birds.

People everywhere were talking about the zoo—and the man behind its success. Steve knew that if he were to venture down the street in America without a bodyguard he would be mobbed, such was the effect of his television series and the film in which he and Terri had starred.

'I can't really move without causing some sort of riot, but that's okay because I can always go home to Beerwah—they don't care about celebrities in Beerwah,' he said. In fact he wasn't keen on the *Crocodile Hunter* series being shown on free-to-air Australian television, worried it would attract the same kind of attention he received in America. 'I was pretty reluctant because I've got to have a little room, you know? I want to be able to go for a surf or go down the shop with no worries.'

The earlier lukewarm response to his film—he was described by one critic as being charmingly disarming in it—did not concern him as much as the ongoing criticism that some expressed about his television wide-eyed 'Crikey!' behaviour. The American television shows won him literally hundreds of millions of fans, but such great success was not without its downside. In Australia the attacks he received were judged to be the effect of the 'tall poppy syndrome'— cutting down those who are successful through either jealousy or because it has been perceived that they do not deserve to have reached a high position in society.

British naturalist, television presenter and author Terry Nutkins savaged Steve by claiming: 'He's put himself up as the star, with animals as extras. It's dreadful television. I don't blow my own trumpet, but I know what I'm talking about.'

Steve was not bothered by such criticism. In fact he hit straight back by announcing that he was to star in a new project that could be operating in no more 'modest' a star-studded place than Las Vegas by early 2007. It was to be a zoo on the famous Strip at which he would perform three croc wrestling shows a day for three months a year. The zoo would be filled with Australian animals such as kangaroos, wallabies, koalas, wombats, snakes—and up to 20 saltwater crocodiles.

The $40 million plan was revealed by John Stainton in Los Angeles at the beginning of 2005 and he said it was hoped the zoo could be situated right in the heart of the Strip, close to some of the world's largest casinos.

'Las Vegas is one of the fastest growing cities in the United States and you have to be on the Strip,' said John. But how would all this fit in with Steve's other activities, including caring for the animals at the Australia Zoo and going off into the outback to relocate crocodiles and collect injured wildlife? John explained that Steve would spend the entire Australian summer at his Queensland zoo and spend three months of the Australian winter in Las Vegas. As for getting the crocodiles to America, Steve, who was excited about the plan, said it would be 'a piece of cake'.

He shifted them all over the place, he said, and referred to the croc he had relocated in Vanuatu, taking it onto the plane virtually unrestrained. But he knew that in Las Vegas he would probably be mobbed by residents, tourists—and stars. He said: 'I'm kind of the stars' star.' He was well aware that there were now several copycats of his dress style on wildlife channels—hosts wearing his trademark khaki shirts and short pants, who tried to copy his enthusiasm. 'Mimics and Steve Irwin look-alikes and wannabes doesn't faze me one iota,' he said. 'Mimicking is the sign of success, it really is.'

Was there something incongruous about a devoted conservationist, a man who went on expeditions into the outback to bond with the creatures of the wild, setting himself up in the world's gambling centre to wrestle crocodiles that he would have to fly in from across the Pacific? On the face of it, it would seem so but Steve might have considered this was yet another means of reaching the masses with his wildlife message—to learn to love all creatures great and small.

In fact that was Steve Irwin, ever the showman, never failing to seize an opportunity. Bizarre as it might have seemed to have a boy from the bush jumping on crocodiles in casino-land, there was no doubt he would have worked hard at sending out the wildlife message, just as he had for so many years.

But it was one ambitious plan that was not to be.

There were others he was looking forward to—buying more land, expanding the zoo, working on more documentaries, searching out corners of the world where species were endangered so he could not only raise the alarm but try to do something about it. Plus there was the exciting prospect of being able to work with his beloved daughter Bindi, who would star in her own wildlife show for children, due to be premiered in the United States in January 2007. A pilot had proved successful, for Bindi, who had watched her father so many times as he worked on his own series, was a natural.

Steve and John Stainton had negotiated a deal in July 2006 with the Discovery Channel to give Bindi a 26-series program called *Bindi, the Jungle Girl*. Her home, like Tarzan's Jane, would be 12 metres (39 feet) up a tree, but it would have rooms and a small bedroom where she sleeps, along with several small animals.

In one crazy scene in which Bindi talks about a koala, Steve can be seen in the background behaving like an orang-outang, swinging backwards and forwards on a rope. In other scenes, the cameras focus on her as she climbs onto elephants and holds a variety of creatures in her hands and arms.

In the following weeks they shot seven episodes, which also involved Steve being on set with his daughter, although it was she who was in the limelight. Steve joked with John that he would be more than happy to be Bindi's co-star.

Steve Irwin had everything to live for as he set off for the Lakefield National Park in August 2006 with his usual team, John Stainton, the camera crew and, of course, his family. Bindi was following in his footsteps in the television world and he was convinced she would become an international star, just like himself. In what was to be his last ever interview in the weeks before, he had told *marie claire* magazine that he had warned Bindi in a big educational message: 'Don't get hurt like your daddy,' he told the magazine, 'because I get hurt a lot.'

He had added in the interview with features editor Jessica Parry that the sun rose and set with Bindi. 'I just long to be with her—I always have, I think I always will.'

As they got muddy in Lakefield National Park, Steve and Terri remained as much in love with one another as the day they had met. He was in a great mood. All the controversies that had embroiled him had become a distant memory. Long gone were the attacks on his showmanship involving Baby Bob and the penguins in Antarctica. It seemed he had been forgiven. His strength of character had withstood the arrows and those who had criticised him had stepped back into the shadows. It was now hard to hurt Steve Irwin, for his growing army of fans were there to protect him.

Queensland Premier Peter Beattie said, before Steve went off to Lakefield National Park, that he wanted Australia to be known for more than someone who just wrestled crocodiles and maybe Steve Irwin could smarten up his image. Outraged fans turned their fury on the premier and he soon made amends by announcing that Steve would be the state's honourary tourism ambassador. Such was the power of Steve's admirers.

The Crocodile Hunter had crashed through it all and now he was back in his little piece of paradise in the Lakefield National Park. It was little wonder he was to tell his friend John Stainton that he was having the best time of his life.

12

The Last Adventure

My field is with apex predators, hence your crocodiles,
your snakes, your spiders ...

It has been their home for tens of millions of years. Huge man-eating crocodiles swim lazily along the rivers in the 50,000 square kilometres that comprise the Lakefield National Park, 200 kilometres north of Cairns.

There are 'freshies'—freshwater crocodiles that are much less dangerous—there too, along with barramundi, butterflies, wallabies, goannas, frilled lizards and dingoes and more than 200 species of birds. In the rainy season the wetlands are mostly inaccessible to the tourists, the fishermen, the birdwatchers and anyone at all interested in wildlife, for all roads and tracks are flooded. The high level of water also increases the danger of crocodile movement. In the dry season rivers become a series of waterholes where crocodiles make their home. It is these places that are particularly dangerous for careless visitors who, sweltering in the humidity, decide to cool off in one of the ponds.

Steve loved the park, for it was his home, too—at least a home away from home. He was comfortable there. The wilderness was his garden. It provided him with an abundance of 'props' for his documentaries. There was always something to train the cameras on, so that Steve could utter his trademark 'Crikey!' and 'Look at this little beauty!' He might point to a rare golden-shouldered parrot or pick up a Lakeland Downs mouse or try to move in close to a spectacled hare-wallaby.

One of the more isolated national parks on the Cape York Peninsula, it was officially gazetted in 1979, for wildlife experts from the Queensland and Federal Governments who carried out extensive research agreed that the region was unique, with its rivers running down to the mangrove-rich coast, the mudflats, vast grasslands and woodlands on the floodplains and the sandstone hills and escarpments. The Old Laura Homestead, lying abandoned in the scrub on the Laura River, gives a clue to the time when brave settlers moved into that crocodile-infested area—the house was built in 1892.

Steve and his team were experts at manoeuvring their 4WD vehicles along and off the rough tracks, steering between magnetic anthills and dodging fallen trees and thick bushes. Without his work, the beauty of the area would never be seen by the rest of the world. But it was more than just aiming a camera at a crocodile, a wombat or a bird. Steve needed to hold his television audience by interacting with the creatures of the wild.

He did not want to risk people turning off because they weren't interested in watching a nature show. He was aware that viewers needed to be transfixed and there was only one way of ensuring that—getting personally involved with an exciting running commentary that took the public along with him as, for example, he crawled on his belly towards a fierce man-eating croc and came face to face with a deadly snake like a taipan. His fans agreed that he was blessed with a natural, indeed uncanny, ability to interact with animals, while his friends referred to that rare and unusual bonding as 'The Force'.

Even in Australia those who knew of Steve's forays into wild places such as Lakefield admired his courage at wrestling with crocodiles to move them to new places for their own sakes but in America it was as if an alien from a distant planet had arrived. Steve Irwin was more than GI Joe, he was braver than Bruce Willis—he was a real live Superman. It was little wonder that Americans could not get enough of him and explained why America's highest-rating talk show, *The Tonight Show* with Jay Leno, asked him to appear no less than 14 times. How he made Leno's audiences laugh when once, when the television host asked him how he determined the sex of a crocodile that was lying on Leno's desk, Steve replied: 'I put my finger in here and if it smiles, it's a girl. If it bites me, it's a boy.' Everybody wanted more of the man in khaki.

Steve had to keep up with the demand. He had to keep travelling. He had to keep filming. He had to keep talking. The pressure was back on, for footage was needed now for Bindi's series.

So it was down to Port Douglas that he and his team travelled to work in a new direction—underwater.

The Great Barrier Reef, as environmentalists, film-makers and tourists had found ever since Captain Cook had first sailed up the east coast of Australia, was a spectacular vein of nature, teeming with exotic creatures that never ceased to fascinate. Consisting of a chain of more than 2800 coral reefs and 900 islands, it stretches south for 2600 kilometres (1615 miles) from the north east coast of Australia and lies in such shallow waters that it can be seen from outer space. Made up of millions of tiny polyps, it was selected as a World Heritage Site in 1981 and because of its accessibility and the exotic fish that dwell among the coral it attracts hundreds of thousands of tourists each year.

They sail out in big craft which moor at various reefs where pontoons with cafeterias have been set up. There is snorkelling to be enjoyed, deep sea diving, or just relaxing in the sun.

On Friday, 1 September, as the big tourist craft threw off their ropes and backed away from the Port Douglas marina, a smaller vessel began its own voyage out to the reef. Its name was *Croc One*, it had the words 'Crocs Rule' painted on the side—and it would be the last time that its owner, Steve Irwin, would leave the mainland.

He stood at the bow in bright sunshine and a lasting image of him shows him playing up to two cameras—waving to one on shore while one of his film crew, who is on the deck with Steve, aims his own camera at the wildlife warrior. For in that brief moment, he was the showman again and this time there was not a single wild species in sight. Just Steve in his khaki shirt and shorts, right leg resting on a rail as he waved towards the shore. It was a poignant, farewell picture, although of course no-one was to realise its significance at the time.

A coroner was expected to examine the events that followed over the next hours but it was the actual circumstances of Steve's tragic death that would come under the microscope. It was routine Steve—get in close—but this time the environment was different. He made sure he manoeuvred himself into the camera shot as he swam with the school of rays, even though the footage was to be used in Bindi's debut television series.

Any kind of wildlife doing anything anywhere—Steve would make sure he captured it on film because he believed it could be used to support any one of his on-screen commentaries. Friends speculated he might have felt perfectly safe swimming close to one of the rays for there had been only two known deaths caused by one of the fish in Australia. They just didn't attack swimmers whose curiosity led them to swim among them.

The incident that killed Steve, however, was different. There was a cameraman in front of the ray which may have caused it to slow and turn. Above was the Crocodile Hunter in his face mask and snorkel, perhaps giving the fish the impression of being trapped. So it struck out and that lethal barb hit Steve in the chest, an action that Bryan Fry of the University of Melbourne's Australian venom research unit likened to a paring knife creating 'a terrific tearing of flesh'. The camera remained trained on Steve—and his friends agreed later that that is what he would have wanted—as he instinctively grabbed the 20 centimetre barb and tore it from his heart, a moment before he lapsed into unconsciousness. That's when the filming stopped. The shocked cameraman guided Steve's body to the surface, yelling for help.

In the hours that followed the frantic attempts to save Steve's life word began to leak out around the country about the tragedy. But not only were first reports vague—they were unbelievable. In fact nobody wanted to believe them. On his afternoon radio show on Sydney's 2UE radio, John Stanley told his listeners that he was hearing reports that a terrible accident had occurred to an iconic Australian figure in the north but he was not prepared to say who it was because if it was wrong it would be just terrible.

Of course, it would be just terrible if it was right, but Stanley was aware there had been other reports over the years of Steve Irwin's untimely death. Within half an hour Stanley was able to tell his listeners that the reports had been confirmed: Steve Irwin was dead.

A stingray? A stingray had killed the man who had so often dodged death in the jaws of man-eating crocodiles? It was unbelievable.

As word spread and tributes began to trickle, then flood in, from shocked fans around the world, marine experts sought to explain how it could have happened. You could die from a barb entering a vital organ—or death could be brought on by the toxic coating on the barb.

In one of the two earlier cases of death, 12-year-old Jeff Zahmel, a north Queensland boy, was speared in the chest by a three-metre (9-foot) ray while fishing on a boat. He spent two days recovering in hospital and was then allowed to go home because the barb had not hit any vital organs. Several days later, his uncle George Zahmel recalled, Jeff finished eating his dinner, stood up 'and dropped dead'. He had died as a result of the stingray's slow-acting poison, his family and doctors unaware that it had been gradually killing his body tissue—a tragic case that later helped to confirm to Steve's friends and family that it was not the poison that had killed him. It seems certain that it was the impact of the barb and the action of pulling it out.

There was agreement among the experts that the ray would have struck out because it was defending itself from a perceived threat. 'They usually don't attack aggressively,' said Dr Mark Meekan, a research scientist at the Australian Institute of Marine Science. 'People usually only get stung by stingrays defending themselves. The tail flips up and over and it will try to stab whatever is attacking it. They are very fast and most people don't see the stingray attack.'

Despite the rare number of deaths, one American study reported that there were some 1500 stingray injuries in America each year, many of them received when people stepped on a hidden ray while walking in shallow water. Victims described the pain as excruciating, one man saying it was like a thousand tarantula spiders biting him.

As Steve's body was lying in the Cairns mortuary and his family and friends led an international outpouring of grief, Australia's cartoon artists paid their own tributes with their pens. An artist with Sydney's *Daily Telegraph* portrayed a large group of sad, stunned animals grouped together with a crocodile saying 'Crikey'. Another

Telegraph cartoon showed a pair of large bush boots standing on a map of the top end of Australia. One empty boot had the words Australian Tourism written on the toe; the other said: Wildlife Conservation. In *The Australian* newspaper two green crocodiles were drawn swimming through a swamp, one wearing a black band on its leg. 'Is the armband a bit much?' it asks.

The flowers piled up outside the zoo gates, three deep, five deep, ten deep. Police were called in to control the traffic. Back at Port Douglas, Steve's crew had a hard decision to make. Should they continue filming? If so, should they go to the very same reef where their friend had died to complete the stingray segment? Is it what Steve would have wanted?

John Stainton believed it was, but the decision to carry on could not be taken by him alone. The film producer was to tell CNN's Larry King, a fan, that they agreed 'to a man' to finish the filming, secretly working for three or four days. John told *Who* magazine: 'It was terrible for all the crew, for everybody involved. I had to ask everyone individually. Two gave me an answer straightaway, others went away for a few hours to think abut it seriously, because this has had such a huge effect on everyone emotionally.'

The decision was to continue filming. 'I don't know how they did it,' said John. 'They were so strong to take on that challenge.' The day after that new round of filming the crew told him they had obtained 'really good vision.' He added: 'The crew said to me the next morning, "Last night, Steve was watching over us for the completion of that shoot. Everything we did went well. The water was like crystal—like a glass house—the animals were there, every-thing was there."'

It was, John said, like a 'copybook shoot'. Poignantly he went on: 'It felt like Steve had a hand in it and he was looking down saying "I am going to make this easier for you all."'

Terri, Steve's father Bob and their closest friends gathered together to discuss Steve's funeral—and burial. News leaked out that the family had been granted special permission to bury the conservationist in the zoo, lying close to the animals that he loved so much. Confirmation appeared to come when television footage from outside the zoo on 9 September showed a white undertaker's van entering the premises with two police escort cars. Friends said Steve had always expressed the wish that if he should die 'anywhere at any time' he would want to be buried at the zoo. Later, when Terri found the strength to describe her agony to interviewer Ray Martin on Channel Nine, she said no-one would ever be told where Steve's resting place was.

Closeted away from the public spotlight and amid great secrecy, a small gathering of family and friends stood together by candlelight at dusk in the zoo for Steve's funeral service. They recounted their fondest memories of the beloved wildlife warrior as the tears flowed.

Later, Steve's dad, Bob said: 'Steve loved having a yarn. Because Steve loved the bush so much and yarning around the campfire, the service was held just like he would have wanted, with everyone telling their favourite stories about him … it now puts some family closure to his life.'

Everyone, it seemed, had so much to say about him that there just wasn't the time.

The family had earlier received offers from the Queensland and Federal Governments for a state funeral, but these were politely rejected because Steve was 'just an ordinary bloke' who would not have wanted such a fuss being made.

The professional that he was, John Stainton held his head high as he paid tribute to his friend at every opportunity. He would tell how Steve might call him at five o'clock in the morning urging him to get up and start working. 'And if you went, you'd have the time of your life because even though the work you were doing was serious, there was always time for laughter,' the film producer said in a tribute he wrote for Australia's *Sunday Telegraph* as preparations were being made for a public memorial service at the zoo on 20 September, 2006.

'We had to look out for each other in different ways. Sometimes, the way he had to look out for me was physical and he saved my life a couple of times. I guess the simplest way to describe how we were was that he looked after me in the bush and I would look after him in the city. In the bush, sometimes he would have to shield me against animals that wanted a piece of me, and in the city I tried to shield him against all the people who wanted a piece of him. I guess it was hardest for him in America, where he literally couldn't leave his hotel room.'

Then in a comment that revealed just how close the two men had been, Stainton added: 'I know this will sound strange to some people: I think he's still with me. I'm still looking out for him and he's still looking out for me. In the past few days when I have struggled, really struggled, to find the right words or make the right decisions, I have felt very strongly that he is with me. When I have sat and cried, I have felt his hand on my shoulder. He's still beside me, still giving me a kick up the bum when I need it.'

There was one thing that John wanted the world to know about his friend of 15 years: he was a man of intellect. That larrikin, happy-go-lucky, rough-and-tumble bloke everyone saw on television was real, 'completely fair dinkum', but Steve was also a deep thinker, a man of great intelligence and a consummate professional. 'I'm just so honoured that in the roller-coaster we took together over all these years, it was me who rode beside him at the end.'

People showed their grief and anger at the way he had died in various ways. While Steve's family and friends retained their tearful dignity, fury turned on the stingray species, with vigilantes searching them out to kill. At least ten stingrays with their tails cut off were found on Queensland beaches. Government officials said they were investigating the deaths and there could be prosecutions for cruelty. This was something that Steve would not have wanted, said his friend Michael Hornby, who is also executive director of Steve's Wildlife Warrior fund. 'We just want to make it very clear that we will not accept and not stand for anyone who's taken a form of retribution,' he said.

'That's the last thing Steve would want. I hope everyone understand we have to protect wildlife now more than ever. This is what Steve was all about.'

13

The Greatest Crocodile Hunter

Even if a big old alligator is chewing me up, I want to go down and go 'Crikey!' just before I die. That would be the ultimate for me.

There is no better place in this age of the Internet to gauge public reaction to the death of Steve Irwin than among the blogs. These messages are the instant, worldwide voices of the people, who even a few years ago might not have bothered to write a letter to their local newspaper or wait in a queue to speak to their radio talk-back host. Their words are unedited. They tell it as they see it, some eloquently, others more clumsily. But their meanings are mostly clear. There is good advice and bad. They lend their support to a topic or dismiss it. They adore a personality or despise him or her.

So how did the world react to the death of Steve Irwin? Here are just a relative few of the literally millions of blogs posted on the Internet.

From the *Sydney Morning Herald* (main points only have been used in some): 'Don't know Steve Irwin but I do know he was a great conservationist purchasing land all over the world for habitat ensuring it couldn't be developed. It is a great loss to our environment but … HYPOCRITES. Anyone who doesn't know as much as he does about animals, in particular crocodiles, has no right to suggest he was endangering his child. Only Steve knows whether he did that or not.'

'Forget his antics. Who cares! He was a great conservationist and that's how he should be remembered.'

'Steve Irwin exemplified the commodification of wildlife. They say there are more tigers in Texas than Asia. In the "Animal Planet" world wildlife only has value if it is dangerous or cuddly. He has been hailed as a great environmentalist and I'm sure he did some good things but we need to value the natural wildlife for its intrinsic rather than entertainment value. Steve's gladiatorial approach to wildlife was successful because the lowest common denominator rules the ratings; see how Sam and the City beats the daily truth. I agree with Greer, nature has had its revenge.'

'He was not a saint, not without his flaws and far from perfect, but from all accounts, he was truly a great Aussie and his death is a tragedy.'

'Praising Steve Irwin for his impressive work towards environmental education and conservation seems to be the latest bandwagon to jump aboard. Flavour of the month.'

'Like him or not, the sad fact is that a little girl has lost the father she adored and a little boy will have little memory of his father. God bless his wife and children. RIP Steve.'

'The public outpouring of grief following his death is, I am sure, honest and well meaning. People feel sorrow for a young man cut down in his prime and in such tragic circumstances. Regardless of personal feelings, Steve Irwin did remind the world to respect and look after animals of all species, shapes and sizes and was much loved for it.'

'I have liked Irwin for many years now. Always thought that he was crazy for sure, but he never said he wasn't. It was refreshing to see someone so into his work. I liked him more once I found out from the head vet at Aussie Zoo that he was the same off camera as he is on.'

'Why is everyone so shocked? The man made a living by playing with deadly animals. It doesn't seem that surprising that "our Steve" would be "snatched away from us" by a dangerous animal.'

'He made me and the kids smile and he did come across as a good bloke who had great passion in his beliefs. He managed to get the point across to children who, let's face it, are the future and I much rather a future where conservation is important.'

When the BBC invited readers of its web page to write in with their reactions to Steve's death the response was so great that the television and radio network said it could not guarantee that everyone's message would be published.

Many, such as these from all around the world, did make it, though:

'May you chase the crocs up in heaven in peace, your family are in our thoughts and prayers, we love your shows and your work, may the legacy you left live long and prosper for many generations.' (Jersey.)

'It was the early morning here in the USA when the news came. I stayed up all night hoping that I had heard wrong … but it was not to be. I've been a fan for years, and my grandkids became fans too. We watched the birth of Bindi … then little Bob. The Croc Hunter was our hero.' (Indiana, USA.)

'It is just an awful tragedy that such a great character as Steve Irwin has passed away in the way that he did … It is just awful watching the repeat programs now knowing that he has passed away. In my opinion there will never be another Steve Irwin.' (Dublin.)

'I have watched the Crocodile Hunter since the beginning. I

had a huge crush on him. He was fantastic to watch, his passion for life. Terri was always by his side and the two of them made great television … My heart breaks every time I see the clips of Bindi and her dad.' (Milwaukee, USA.)

'Irwin is a bloke with a character bigger than any modern environmentalist and a true naturalist. He has contributed to many wildlife conservation action through his life not only in Aussie but throughout the world. His television show is breathtaking, showing how many really can live alongside the wild as long as there is an understanding made between them.' (Bangkok, Thailand.)

'Gosh, I really can't believe it, the death of Steve Irwin. He was such a hero to me. I looked up to him from when I was six to this day (I'm 16). He truly has made a difference in this world we live in … You know I thought for sure sometime in my life I was going to meet Steve. I thought I just had to, but that's all changed.' (Los Angeles.)

'I watched him for years on his shows, almost felt like I knew him personally. I feel like someone in my family has died.' (Quitman, MS USA.)

'An honesty of soul, conviction and generosity. Not just an Australian, although a great one at that, but an icon to the world. His legacy will live on for generations. Sadness will embrace the world, Steve Irwin, but the memory of your passion will be here for ever.' (Adelaide, Australia.)

'Two children and a wife have lost a good man. They will miss him long after the news dies down. He was so full of passion for animals and people listened to him and wanted to back his ideas and I hope his ideals never die … .he is one of the good guys.' (Glasgow).

'When there are so many evil people alive on this planet, why is it that those who do nothing but good are taken from us?...The world has lost a great teacher …' (Tennessee.)

An American website called the *Blog of Death*, which despite its macabre-sounding name runs tributes to people who have died, no matter what their fame or otherwise, was flooded with tributes to the Crocodile Hunter. Messages reveal how many people regarded Steve as part of their family:

'I always enjoyed watching Steve and his fascinating relationship with the animals. He taught my family what it means to respect and love all the animals of the wild.'

'Steve was my idol … I have pictures of all of the family.'

'I thought that I was strange, feeling the way that I do. I've been talking to my boss … not caring what happens to me. I don't really care what happens to me anymore. It feels like life is over as I knew it. I feel that I have lost my best friend and I can't go on anymore.'

'Steve made the ultimate sacrifice for us. His death was no accident. It was a message sent via the stingray to us. Let's pay attention. 'We are all too complacent about our environment and extinction due to habitat loss. It's too easy to sit around watching your high definition television in your air conditioned house watching "nice" civilised environmentalists that stay far away from animals telling you how great they live in the wilderness. What wilderness? Most of those films take place in wilderness preserves … Steve really wrestled with the problem of conservation and was dangerously close to the problem ironically, and placed himself in harm's way to make a point, to make us pay attention. Some might think the stingray got him because he was taking revenge on Steve, but those of us that think there are other forces in nature, of a higher order, might think the stingray killed him so that Steve could make the ultimate sacrifice for the sake of our environment and these animals, so we may finally pay attention and take notice.'

From South Africa, Samantha Thorburn revealed the powerful influence Steve had had on her life: 'I first saw Steve Irwin on television years ago as a very young girl. I loved watching his adventures, I loved his passion for wildlife and conservation. And I adored his quirky sense of humour and Aussie lingo. He was one of my biggest influences and I can say one of the reasons why I went ahead and studied nature conservation. I had lived and worked in the bush for many years as a conservationist and it is always an absolute tragedy when "one of us" is lost. It is an honour to say that he brought conservation and the importance of our natural heritages and wildlife to the fore.'

Evidence that people saw Steve as a friend or even a family member continued to pour in to blogs around the world, even though many people admitted they knew him only through his shows:

'I didn't know Steve Irwin that well and only watched a few of his shows, but I feel a deep love and admiration for him and everything he stood for and an emptiness knowing I'll never see anything new from him. I hope Terrie and her children do something in the media to fill the void. It just doesn't make sense and never will to me of his untimely death. Another magnet on the other side that is pulling us to the other side to be with them.'

'This has affected my family more than I could have imagined; he has been a great influence on myself and my two boys. The world will never be the same ... Steve falls under the obvious category of Hero.'

There were messages, too, from India. Abira Banerjee wrote from West Bengal: 'I must admit when I first saw The Croc Hunter on Discovery Channel, I thought he is crazy! After seeing some of the episodes, the movie and the talkshow I started to love seeing Steve in fearless action. I think Steve is the best. It is inspiring how passionate he is about his career. Steve is very brave ... He taught me what it means to love all the animals of the wild and the tame also.'

'Steve Irwin will be missed by all conservationists who want to preserve wildlife. After the memorials and accolades are over, we need to carry on his legacy in our own small ways. If every Steve Irwin fan would make a small donation to a wildlife organisation, it would make a big difference. Wildlife is disappearing worldwide except in Australia where Steve bought large tracts of land. People also need to have a heightened awareness about wildlife; and not only the cute and cuddly ones like the panda. That is Steve's legacy; he showed us that ALL wildlife is important, even those animals that are feared, like snakes.'

'my name is Shannon and I'm 11 years old. i wish you didn't have to go. you were my idol. i looked up to you. well at least you died doing something you loved. you will be missed by tons of people. i wish you didn't leave us steve. you were the greatest crocodile hunter. i miss you so much.'

Yes, it was children around the world who were affected by Steve's death as much as their parents and conservationists. As television networks in Australia and America announced they would provide live coverage of the memorial service that was being arranged, Australia's Education Department examined the effect that such a moving event would have on youngsters, already saddened by his death. An extraordinary decision was reached—before children would be allowed to watch the event on television at their schools a note from their parents would be required.

Sydney's *Daily Telegraph* reported it had been told by sources that officials were worried the service might be too traumatic for thousands of youngsters, already distressed by the Crocodile Hunter's death. Sue Ingram, president of the Primary Principals' Association, said Steve was the 'children's hero' and his death had a huge effect on children. However, there were feelings by experts that allowing children to watch might be an opportunity to talk to children about death. Former teacher Judith Locke, who is now a clinical psychologist, said she could not imagine the service being in poor taste or being a shock to children.

'It's an excellent learning opportunity. While it's a sad situation, it's part of the cycle of life,' she said.

At his home in Sydney's Marrickville, five-year-old Kai Hardge, was finishing off a drawing of a crocodile he planned to send to the zoo, with a farewell message. 'I loved Steve Irwin,' he said. 'He was my best friend. I wish I could have met him properly. I hope they put some more of his old shows on television because I'm going to watch every one.'

His mother, Carla Hardge, said: 'When Steve was on television you wouldn't have been able to tear Kai away if the house was on fire.'

It had been one of the most shocking periods in Australian history. First had come Steve's bizarre death, followed by the death just four days later of a second major figure, motor racing champion Peter Brock, who was killed, like Steve, in his line of work.

Aged 61, Brock was known as the King of the Mountain, for the number of times he had won a mountain car race at Bathurst, NSW. On 8 September he died from his injuries when his rally car smashed into a tree during a race in Western Australia. In words that echoed those of Steve's friends, Brock's long-time friend Allan Moffat said: 'He was doing what he loved to do.

'But even so, it beggars belief that one week can claim two great Australians icons—both too young.'

How was the nation going to cope with a big memorial for service for Steve and a funeral for Peter in the same week? In a magnanimous gesture, the Irwin family said they would hold off on Steve's memorial service until after the farewell to Peter, a state funeral which had been offered and accepted by his family.

Planning for Steve's memorial, in the wake of that earlier private funeral service in the zoo, went ahead amid speculation that it might be held in a large stadium in Queensland. But Steve's family and friends agreed that Steve would want it held in the zoo grounds.

Flags flew at half mast on the Sydney Harbour Bridge as Brock's funeral went ahead in Melbourne, the emblems marking the deaths of both Peter and Steve, and they were to remain in place until after the memorial for Steve.

The Premier of NSW, Mr Morris Iemma, said: 'Both Peter Brock and Steve Irwin made a magnificent contribution to our country and we are all the poorer for their passing. Peter Brock was a nine-time winner of the Bathurst 1000 who helped put Bathurst on the international motor racing map, and Steve Irwin was a much-loved ambassador for Australian wildlife and a passionate conservationist. On behalf of everyone in NSW who has been entertained, educated and enthralled by the contributions of Peter Brock to motor sport and Steve Irwin to conservation, we pay tribute in our small way to these two magnificent Australians.'

When it was announced that 3000 free tickets would be made available at ticket outlets in Brisbane and at the zoo, people queued through the night to ensure they did not miss out. They were all gone within 15 minutes. Many of those who failed to get tickets simply wept.

14

A Man Who Changed the World

There's only one way to shoot a crocodile, and that's with a camera.

No greater tribute can be given to a man than to have the world—his peers, families, children, government leaders, internationally known television hosts and Hollywood stars and entertainers—united in a simple chorus of praise like that given to the larrikin from the bush. For Steve Irwin, doing what he did best, had changed their world.

From every corner of the globe came the adulation on Wednesday, 20 September 2006, as all who had known him, either personally or through his documentaries, said goodbye with their words and silent tears. But the most poignant, lingering, moment at the memorial service at the Australia Zoo on that sunny Wednesday morning came when eight-year-old Bindi stood confidently before a crowd of 5000, dwarfed by a huge image of her father, and told of her love for him—and her vow to continue his work.

Bindi, with poise and courage, took grief in her stride and left no-one in any doubt that not only was she prepared to follow in her father's footsteps, but she had the ability to do it. The Crocoseum rose to its feet in a standing ovation for both the Crocodile Hunter and his tiny daughter.

John Stainton, who had orchestrated the remarkable global farewell so that even those in some hidden reaches of the world could share that final journey with his friend and their hero, had already signalled that the Crocodile Hunter's legacy would never die. The mantle would pass to his television-savvy daughter who was the prime candidate to ensure the show went on.

She was a child already in advance of her years and if anyone thought she was far too young to even consider getting on with the job of spreading the wildlife gospel according to her father, those doubts were soon dispelled as she read her moving tribute to him.

We cannot call them mourners, that huge crowd of VIPs and ordinary folk who flocked to the zoo that day, for no-one wanted to grieve over the passing of a man who deserved a grand celebration of his life; rather, the crowds who wanted to stand as close as possible to Terri and her family at the zoo were in a joyous mood, despite the emotions that were soon to overwhelm them.

In the 16 days since Steve died, his freakish death had been talked about everywhere, not just in Australia but around the world. Many youngsters who watched his shows said they were now looking forward to seeing Bindi on television and were going to do something to remember Steve by, too. At Sydney's Bexley North Primary School, children had already begun work on their own special Crocodile Hunter memorial garden, consisting of a frog pond and native plants. Mark Meecham, the school Principal, said the students had reacted enthusiastically to the idea of setting up the garden to help overcome their sadness. 'We decided we should focus on the positive aspects of Steve's life as a way of helping the children to cope,' he said.

Crowds had started to gather at the zoo many hours before the memorial service. One woman, from the Sydney suburb of Leichhardt, had driven the 1000 kilometres (620 miles) to Beerwah, parking outside the night before and sleeping in her car to ensure that, even though she had secured one of the rare tickets that had been issued, she would get a good seat at the ceremony. Holli Durban flew in from California with her 13-year-old daughter Brittani hoping for tickets. A local woman, feeling sorry for her, gave up her own tickets for the American visitors.

A large corps of police were called in for traffic duty as streams of cars travelled along Glasshouse Mountains Road, their drivers gazing up at Steve's face on the gigantic roadside billboards promoting his zoo. Car radios carried up-to-date reports of the scene outside the zoo, hours before the service was due to begin. There was so much interest in covering the event by media representatives from around the world that the zoo was forced to keep most journalists outside, asking them to watch the proceedings on television monitors.

There were hundreds, if not thousands, of khaki shirts, some of them bearing scrawled ink messages to Steve … 'Crikey! A word we will never forget', 'Steve, we will never forget you … ' 'A true Australian … '

The memorial service was to be beamed live around the world, to all the major television networks. There had been a military coup in Thailand and the plug had been pulled on all television programs but nothing could stop the Steve Irwin broadcast—apart from state media the only show reaching into Thai homes was the memorial service.

Such was the fame that Steve had achieved that television hosts fought for the right to interview Terri at some time in the near future—a fierce battle that was eventually won by the grand dame of American interviewers, Barbara Walters. Australia's top television identity, Ray Martin, was also granted the privilege. But there were many more stars who wanted to reach out a comforting arm to the family, if only in spirit, or perhaps snatch the chance to whisper a 'good luck'.

Terri, too distraught to take an active part of the ceremony or to say any words, sat with her arms around her children. Bindi stroked her mother's hair, a tiny tower of strength.

It began, that wonderful celebration of Steve's life, with an internationally broadcast tribute from his close friend Russell Crowe, speaking from New York. Dressed in a dark suit and black tie, Russell stood in a garden as he talked sombrely and, at times, directly to the friend he had lost.

'It was way too soon and completely unfair on all accounts,' he said, his voice breaking. 'I know as humble as you always were, you would still be pleased to know that the world sends its love and that people all over this planet have been grieving. We have all lost a friend, we have lost a champion and we are going to take some time to adjust to that.'

Then as if addressing Steve through the camera he said: 'I'm in New York, mate, the big city, where you have been headline news … you've been headline news on CNN for a week. There's not many zookeepers who would command that sort of attention, mate, and all that means is that you got the message across. You got the word out there and you were heard and you will be remembered.'

On big screens in shopping centres around Queensland and in millions of homes around the world, scenes were shown of Steve sparring with Charlie the crocodile at the zoo, water splashing everywhere as he dodged the snapping jaws. One of those watching the memorial on a large screen on the Sunshine Coast were friends Karen Richardson and Dianne Landamore. 'I never knew him but it was like he was my brother,' said Karen. 'I can't get over he's gone. I just can't accept it. I wasn't this upset when my grandfather passed away.'

Dianne was equally upset by Steve's death. 'It was hard losing Princess Diana and Elvis, but with Steve, he was part of us.'

At the Crocoseum, a big amphitheatre where Steve would put on his crocodile shows, Prime Minister John Howard stepped forward to pay a personal tribute to a man he genuinely admired.

'My fellow Australians,' he said, speaking without notes, 'we gather in this special place that Steve created to celebrate the life of a remarkable man and a remarkable Australian. Steve Irwin touched the heart of Australians and touched the heart of millions around the world in a very special way.

'He did that because he had that quality of being genuine, of being authentic, of being unconditional, of having a great zest for life and throughout his all-too-short life he demonstrated a love for the two things that ought to matter more to all of us than anything else—his love of his family and his love of his country.'

The Prime Minister's voice broke slightly as he continued: 'He brought to Australians and the world an understanding of nature. He taught children in particular to love and respect all creatures great and small. In everything he did, he was direct, he was genuine and oh-so Australian and that is what we loved so much about him.'

Again there was a catch in his voice before he added some personal words for Steve's family: 'Can I say, to you, Terri, to Bob and to Bob and to Bindi and to all the other members of the Irwin family—we grieve with you but we celebrate this remarkable life, this life that projected Australia in such a robust, hopeful way to the rest of the world.

'And as we share this celebration and we honour this life and I say to you Terri and the rest of this family, there are 20 million pairs of Australian arms reaching out to embrace you this morning and to express our love and respect for what your beloved Steve in his 44 years gave to Australia, gave to the creatures of this earth and gave to the world.'

The praise from the Prime Minister would have been more than enough for the family of anyone whose life was being celebrated, but there was so much more to come, for there was so much more to be said about the Wildlife Warrior. One of Steve's favourite folk singers was John Williamson and up he stepped with his guitar, sleeves rolled up, to sing one of the conservationist's favourite songs. The words could have been written specially for the occasion:

'Hey True Blue, don't say you're gone, say you've stepped out for a smoko, and you'll be back later on … '

Cameras panned the crowd. Adults and children, many wearing khaki, were weeping. But then, as the song ended, people erupted in cheers. The significance of the words had not been missed.

Anthony Field of the children's entertainers The Wiggles, who have worked with Steve in educating children about the wild, stood in the zoo's Crocoseum and recalled how Steve had built the zoo from a humble reptile park that had been started by his dad Bob and his mum Lyn—a memory which provoked applause from the crowd.

'He transformed it into one of Australia's "must-see" destinations,' said Anthony. 'Steve designed and built this magnificent Crocoseum so that he could showcase the reptiles he loved so much.'

But this was not a memorial service in which only Australians were playing a part. Onto the screens came the face of Cameron Diaz, speaking from America. 'People were just taken by him,' she said. 'Just inspired and in awe of his energy and how he went about putting himself forward and what he represented. And America, every kid, was in love with the idea of just being him.'

'Steve,' said Anthony Field, 'grew up among the wildlife that he cared about so passionately and there was no stopping him from getting in among the snakes and crocs right from his earliest years. Through television documentaries and his shows here at Australia Zoo he became a man of action, who captured the world.'

Then there was Steve on the screen, grasping snakes, dodging crocs, swimming with sharks, mingling with seals. A segment of film showed him catching a large crocodile in a net. 'I spent what felt like a lifetime up in the wilderness catching crocodiles on my own,' he said into the camera. 'And occasionally I have family and friends helping me. Which was great. Dad bought me this old National video recorder which I used to capture everywhere a piece of history.' He showed off a bleeding ankle: 'Look what that crocodile did to me!' he exclaimed—then looking affectionately at the reptile said: 'Thanks a lot!'

One of Steve's closest friends, who had spent years travelling into the outback with him on a variety of adventures—and who once received a nasty croc bite on the leg for his troubles—is Wes Mannion, director of Australia Zoo. When he introduced himself he was given a warm welcome, for many had heard that he and Steve had worked well together.

'I was naturally drawn to Australia Zoo and as a 14-year-old boy could not wait to visit,' he said. 'I expected a place full of beautiful and fascinating creatures and I was not disappointed. Australia Zoo was an amazing place, a place where reptiles and wildlife reigned supreme. Where creatures that were persecuted and hated because of human ignorance and misunderstanding were loved and nurtured.

'That first day I visited I knew I had found my calling. I expected many things that day but nothing could have prepared me for the man I was about to meet.' The camera moved around to Terri, sitting in her khakis her arm wrapped around young Bob, Bindi sitting beside her sipping from a bottle of water.

'His name was Steve,' Wes continued. 'Steve's enthusiasm was instantaneously infectious. His love and passion for wildlife was so enveloping that at the time I found it difficult to breathe. His natural ability with wildlife was extraordinary. We hit it off immediately and from that moment on my life became a montage of adventure and excitement.

'He wanted to teach me everything he could as fast as he could. I guess he needed to fast-track my skills. It was as if somehow he knew there was so much to achieve in such a short amount of time and that he needed to surround himself with like-minded people who had a passion for wildlife and its protection.

'I will never forget the first day he let me feed my first croc. Steve had waited impatiently for his mum and dad to leave the zoo on a field trip.' To laughter from those listening in the zoo auditorium, Wes continued: 'The moment we waved goodbye Stevo said, "Hey mate, it's about time you fed Anvil." Anvil was a 3½-metre (14-foot) saltwater crocodile.' Steve's father Bob smiled behind his dark glasses as Wes continued his story.

'I said'—and then he put on a squeaky voice—"you bet, mate". I was only 15 at the time so my voice hadn't quite broken. I fed Anvil without a hitch and I will never forget his beaming smile that day ...' His memories overwhelming him, he paused to compose himself. Then added: 'He was so proud. It did not matter if I was catching crocs in Northern Australia or venomous snakes in Africa. If Stevo was nearby I felt I could achieve anything. He had that effect on the people around him. Over time we continued to grow closer and closer and shared so many exciting times. As the years have gone by I have watched Steve find the woman of his dreams, seen the world fall for Steve's enthusiastic love of wildlife as I had as a young boy, seen Australia Zoo become one of the best zoos in the world, but by far his greatest achievement has been as a dad.'

RICHARD SHEARS

It was difficult for Wes to continue, but he managed it. 'His love and dedication to his children has been inspiring. He was a true natural. Steve has become my brother, mentor, and best mate. To the world he was a hero. To me he was my hero. He saved my life. I'll miss you, mate.'

On the big screen behind him, footage was rolling, showing a crocodile grabbing him by the leg. But Steve had managed to free him and pull him from its jaws. There were pictures of Wes lying in hospital with gaping bite wounds to his leg, but Steve is heard to say, lightheartedly: 'He made a full recovery. He made a full recovery really quick.'

Australian singer Daniel McGahan stood on the back of Steve's pick-up truck to sing of how 'He changed our world; to change this world you need the heart of a lion, the faith of a child … . To change this world … crikey, what a venture … You changed my world …'

The face was instantly recognisable. He appeared on the screen in his trademark braces and blue shirt, finger pointing at the camera to get his point across. Larry King, CNN's interviewing giant, joined the line-up of the world's notable identities to heap praise on the Australian conservationist.

'I loved having him on my show, not just because he was terrific television but because he impressed my two youngest sons, Chance and Cannon,' he said. 'I've interviewed presidents, kings and Oscar winning movie stars. My boys just shrugged.

'But once I talked to the real-life, world-famous croc hunter, well, that made me a hero. Steve's connection with kids will be one of his enduring legacies. He took 'em to the animal world up close and personal. He gave them education as well as excitement

'To Steve's wife, Terri, my sincere condolences. To Steve's children, Bindi, Bob, your dad was a great man. He made this world a better place. We'll miss him a lot.'

Professor Craig Franklin, one of the world's leading crocodile biologists, told the crowd that he felt privileged because he had spent the previous month of August with Steve in the far north of Queensland, in the Lakefield National Park, along with Steve's family and what he described as Steve's phenomenal Australia Zoo croc team.

It was not a filming trip, but a research expedition that had the support of the Australian Research Council. What was not generally known, he said, was that Steve was a driving force behind a project in which satellite transmitters and dive recorders were attached to the largest saltwater crocodiles Steve could catch.

For a number of years, said Professor Franklin, researchers had been tracking these crocodiles from space and had discovered they undertake many voyages of hundreds of kilometres, including trips out to the Great Barrier Reef, and they can dive for in excess of two hours.

'These are all new scientific discoveries that Steve has a big part of,' he explained, speaking in the current tense as if he, like so many others, had not accepted Steve Irwin's death.

'Steve brought to the research project his vast knowledge about crocodiles, his world renowned expertise in catching them and his passion to learn more about these remarkable animals. While not formally trained as a scientist, he had all the qualities of a great scientist. He was driven by curiosity and he had an endless list of questions that he sought answers to.'

Then Professor Franklin revealed just how highly academics revered Steve's work—in recognition of his standing and contribution to science, he said, the University of Queensland had been about to appoint him as an adjunct professor—he would have become Professor Steve Irwin. The news was greeted with cheers from the crowd, many with tiny Australian flag tattoos on their faces.

'Steve was simply inspiring to work with,' said the Professor, laying to rest any suggestion that the Crocodile Hunter was all show. 'He strongly believed that the more information he could find out about crocodiles and share with the world, the better we would understand, appreciate and protect them. His outward expression, passion and love of animals great and small has empowered us all to be wildlife warriors and protectors of the environment. This is the legacy that Steve Irwin leaves behind and one all of us must continue for future generations.'

Steve broke a finger and cracked a rib when he attached a satellite receiver to one crocodile—and the world saw the footage as it was replayed during the memorial service. He didn't care about his injures. 'I feel good—my mission is complete!' he declared.

In his forays into the outback, Steve often spoke to Aboriginal people on whose land he wanted to work. He always respected their culture and now, at his memorial service, the love that the indigenous people had for him was brought to the fore.

'Steve,' explained Anthony Field of The Wiggles, 'always had a great respect for the land and its traditional owners. Over the years and through his many adventures Steve always set aside time for the indigenous people who shared his love and respect for the creatures who make up their natural world.'

Then he introduced the Aboriginal people who had risen in the crowd— the matriarch of the Gubbi Gubbi people, whose land includes the remarkable Glasshouse Mountains, Dr Eve Fesl and her sons. The men stood bare chested, daubed in traditional white paint, as Dr Fesl, whose expertise at the Queensland University of Technology is in indigenous studies, linguistics and Aboriginal ethnography, spoke first in her tribal tongue.

Then she recited the moving translation 'for Steve':

'At dawn, the magpies sing and by day the black cockatoo wing their way across a sunny sky. The koala, possum, dingo and carpet snake are silent on the land below. A mist covers the mountains. We and our lands are crying for you. Steve, you jumped, laughed and worked for us. Thank you, good on you, Steve. Hear our call for you … We join now with the people here in sending the ancient call of the Gubbi Gubbi and the modern call of the Australian bush, which has been adopted. We call across the world to you and we want you to join us.'

Everyone present at the zoo that morning knew what she meant. On the count of three there was a united cry of: 'Cooooeeeeeee!'

Steve had been a guest on all the big-time radio and television shows in America, including the morning show hosted by Steve Harvey, voted one of America's funniest and most popular comics.

There was a clip of the Australian in the studio listening to the black host telling his listeners: 'The Crocodile Hunter, everybody, is from Australia.' Turning to Steve he said: 'I would like to commend you for your speed and agility … You are so real, cat, to me, right now, you are officially black.' Steve roared with laughter and said: 'Thanks mate. You have no idea how much I appreciate that. I'm just this bloke in Australia doing my thing and that goes straight to my heart.'

Then a new but very familiar face appeared on television screens around the world as part of the memorial service. It was a pre-recorded and incisive tribute to Steve from Kevin Costner:

'His son and daughter and his wife can be very proud that not only was their father seemingly, to the rest of the world, fearless that he would be around these animals, I think where he is the most fearless is that he let us see who he was. And that is being brave in today's society, because when you show yourself there are so many people willing to mimic you, to mock you, and he was unafraid of that—because he knew that his idea, his truth was a lot bigger than the aside joke.'

John Stainton, best mate, producer, director, manager and partner stood up. He really needed no introduction, although that was how he presented himself to those who had gathered at the zoo. He wanted to share with everyone, he said, the way in which Steve changed his life for ever. From the time they first met, they clicked: the khaki-clad wildlife warrior and the city slicker became the best of friends over 20 odd years—'and they were odd'.

Everyone knew the Steve who was in front of the camera. What people didn't know was that Steve was behind the camera as well, filming those tricky, dangerous shots which transformed all of their documentaries into what was 'must-watch' television shows.

To support his words, John presented clips of Steve working behind the camera, offering to cook lunch for the croc crew. He was seen with a camera filming very close to the jaws of a crocodile, an alligator and a snake that was trying to bite him.

'As you can see,' said John, 'you can always rely on Steve to get the best shots and the dangerous ones at that. But in front of the camera, Steve was the ultimate professional.' That was a jokey comment as John presented The Best Picture Show Company's blooper clips of Steve getting his words muddled as he addressed the camera and shots of him falling out of a tree, tripping over fences, and getting a drenching as he tumbled from a dingy.

'Steve was a true, fair dinkum Aussie and his way with words and his command of the Australian language made me very proud,' said John, bringing smiles as he showed film of Steve making curious noises—'Whack! Bang! Whoooo!'

Actress and talk show host Kelly Ripa said in a pre-recorded tribute to Steve: 'He embraced and captured the imagination of certainly my kids and myself included. I mean, he really had such a passion for what he did and enjoyed every day of his life so much. You could feel it—it was infectious, you know, and I was so grateful. Even though I had four or five brief encounters with Steve it will take me through the rest of my life. I will never forget him.'

Despite the passion he had for getting to know the unknown, said Anthony from The Wiggles, his heart was always here in the land of the gum trees. It was a cue, of course, for John Williamson to step forward—or rather to stand up on the back of Steve's truck—and sing his famous song: 'Give me a home among the gum trees … '

The moving memorial celebration, unprecedented in its world-wide reach and for the number of international VIPs who poured out their praise, heard next from Clark Bunting from the Discovery Channel on which Steve was a major star.

He was yet another who said he was privileged to be a friend of Steve's. When he first met him, he said in a recording that was beamed around the world, it was as the head of a brand new cable channel in America—Animal Planet. He had always believed that television networks were defined by who they put on the air. When he and his colleagues started the channel they were hoping to find someone who would change the way about how people felt about animals and nature.

'And then I saw Steve. Even though it was a very rough video tape, his passion sincerity and knowledge were obvious. I remember thinking to myself, "If this guy is for real we have to work with him."

'Anyone who spent any time with Steve knew that above all else he was real. He was really, really real. Steve knew instinctively that television's greatest power isn't so much that it can tell you what to think but it most certainly can tell you what to think about. And he did that better than anyone I have ever seen by concentrating on, focusing on, conservation and education.

'In education, Steve wasn't some sort of academic dry exercise; instead he would reach to the television and grab us all by the lapels, pulls us all through the screen and we were all standing three feet behind him.' It could be, said Clark Bunting, looking at the prehistoric beauty of a saltwater croc or the majesty of a black mambo. 'He helped us observe the world through his unique and wonderful perspective. This was his true magic. This was a life incredibly well lived.'

It may have been one of the hardest things he had to do in his life, but Steve's father, Bob, made his way to the microphone. While he had been smiling at the recollections of his son's adventures, this was the moment when he had to pay a public farewell to him before a worldwide audience of hundreds of millions. He kept it simple.

'On behalf of Terri, Bindi and Bob, and my two girls Mandy and Joy, I would like to thank all of you for your kind thoughts and letters, flowers and sympathy. Please don't grieve for Steve. He is at peace now.

'But I would like you to grieve for the animals; the animals who have lost the best friend they ever had. And so have I.

'I was fortunate to just recently spend three or four weeks with Steve on crocodile research and he was the best he had been for many years. And I will certainly treasure that.' That was all he wanted to say.

It was fitting that at that moment a clip of Steve and his dad on a crocodile hunt was shown. Steve heaps praise on his father. 'My dad was my hero, my mentor and he was sort of ahead of his time with wildlife,' he says in the video. 'He was at the cutting edge of animal husbandry and understanding the wilderness and all of the wildlife in it.' There were shots of Steve catching a croc with his father after which he tells Bob: 'It's been a real honour sharing this with you, mate.'

His dad says: 'We're a good team, you and me.'

Then Steve recalls: 'I was born on my mum's birthday, so every time my birthday comes around I just get this overwhelming warmth that engulfs my whole body.

'The devastation of losing my mum knocked the wind out of me for over a year. Anyone who has lost someone who is that close to you will always carry that pain. You can cut my arm off, you can cut my legs off, but when you lose a family member like that it hurts you, it devastates you forever, but you know you owe [it to] that person to get back up and stride ahead and try harder. You have just got to get up there, got to keep going.'

Prime Minister Howard had already paid tribute to Steve but there was more to come from government circles. Senator Ian Campbell quickly explained his role: 'If you are Australia's environment minister, how lucky could you be to know Steve Irwin.'

He went on: 'Steve became known around our world as a deeply committed, very practical and down to earth conservationist. He taught all of us so much about our unique wildlife and its Australian habitat. He made the environment a mainstream issue, not just the preserve of a small handful of activists.

'Steve's public environmental work was incredibly well known. What amazed me was that he did more in private than in public. Transformational stuff. His massive personal investment in conservation reserves. He pioneered one of the great movements in modern environmentalism in Australia, the private nature park. His crocodile research using space age satellite tracking systems to monitor estuarine crocs, guiding our management for them into the future.'

He added more achievements to the list: 'Steve's dedication to global issues, from his work to save precious habitat for threatened elephants in Asia to his incredibly strong encouragement and support for the Australian government's efforts to bring an end to the whale slaughter.

'Steve's infectious enthusiasm for our wildlife entered living rooms around our planet and transformed the way we all relate to nature. In changing the way we all think, he has changed the way we act, and that is the single greatest gift he has given us all. How this and future generations care for our environment will never be the same. The world is a much better place for Steve's all-too-short stay. I am a very lucky man to have known him.'

Steve sat with an orang-outang and her baby in a new clip. 'The emotions I felt in my heart to be loved by this beautiful mummy orang,' he said in the recording. There was an adoring shot of him with a baby elephant, its tiny trunk searching out the profile of his face.

More. There was another big name from the entertainment industry. Singer Justin Timberlake spoke this time: 'To Terri and Bindi and Bob, Steve's family and friends … you know, I may have only maybe spent a day with you guys but it was a day I'll never forget and I'll never forget what I learned, just by being around Steve. Not even what he taught me but what I learned from just being around him with animals. My thoughts and prayers are with all of you and he will definitely be missed.'

Yet for all the stars who had spoken there was one more voice to be heard. The words were simple, but the message was the most powerful to spread out to the world that morning. She was so small, standing as she did in front of the giant photo of her father. She should have been afraid. So many people. But Steve's daughter, waiting for the calls of 'We love you, Bindi' to die down spoke with courage and self-assurance.

'My daddy was my hero,' she said, reading from a single sheet of paper, her right finger tracing the words. 'He was always there for me when I needed him. He listened to me and taught me so many things, but most of all he was fun.

'I know that daddy had an important job. He was working to change the world so everyone would love wildlife like he did. He built a hospital to help animals and he bought lots of land to give animals a safe place to live. He took me and my brother and my mum with him all the time.'

Bindi spoke joyously. She had a smile on her face as she told how she and her father caught crocodiles together and how much she loved being in the bush with him. 'I don't want daddy's passion to ever end. I want to help endangered wildlife, just like he did. I had the best daddy in the whole world and I will miss him every day.

'When I see a crocodile I will always think of him. And I know that daddy made this zoo so that everyone could come and learn to love all the animals. Daddy made this place his whole life. Now it's our turn to help daddy. Thank you.'

With that, and a soft smile, she turned and walked back to her mother, who had sat tearfully listening to her brave child, an arm around her son Bob.

They cheered, they applauded, they gave her a standing ovation. She was her daddy's little girl. Then Wes Mannion was back. Steve had a passion for all wildlife, he said, but he simply fell in love with elephants and his three favourite 'girls'—his favourite 'ellies'—at the zoo were Siam, Sabu and Bimbo. He loved them so much, said Wes, that they could do no wrong if they walked through the zoo. If the elephants started ripping apart and eating the zoo's palm trees, Steve would say, 'No, no, it's okay, they can have 'em.' The gardeners would just go crazy, said Wes.

As he spoke, the elephants were led out. They were going to be fed by Steve's father, Bob, by Bindi, and Steve's older sister Joy—just as Steve liked to do.

Bindi ducked and weaved when an elephant playfully ran the tip of its trunk around her face as she fed it. Wes smiled at the scene and went on: 'Steve's passion for elephant conservation has spanned from tsunami-ravaged Banda Aceh through to supporting conservation projects throughout the fragile ecosystems of South East Asia. Elephants will always be in our hearts here at Australia Zoo.'

Another giant from the entertainment world appeared on the screen: Hugh Jackman, who played Wolverine in *X-Men* and its sequels and portrayed the life of singer Peter Allen in *The Boy from Oz*.

'Steve is not here with us in body, but in spirit,' he said. 'He will always be here. When I spoke with my son a few days ago he said to me, "Daddy I think we should all be warriors like Steve." I just said to him, "You're absolutely right." So whether it's for the wilderness, whether it's for the animals, his family, or whether it's for just the planet or just life in itself, Steve showed us that we live like warriors and we make the world a better place.'

Actor David Wenham, who had had a role in Steve's feature film, read a poem by Rupert McDavid, 'The Crocodiles Are Crying'. 'Yes he was a lunatic, yes he went in head first, but he made the world happy with his energetic burst … As sure as Crikey fills the sky, I think we'll miss you, Steve, goodbye … '

There were final words from Steve on that big screen. 'Come with me,' he said. 'Share my wildlife with me, because humans want to save things that they love. My job, my mission, the reason I've been put onto this planet, is to save wildlife and I thank you for coming with me. Yeah, let's get 'em!'

It was time to escort Steve—or at least his spirit—from his beloved Crocosoreum.

For what was described as his 'last research trip into the great unknown', Brian Coulter, his 'right hand croc man', was given the privilege of driving Steve's truck out of the zoo on its final journey past a guard of honour made up of all his croc crew.

First they ceremoniously and carefully packed onto the back all his usual gear—swags, ropes, a cooler box, picks, shovels, nets, and finally, his surfboard. John Williamson sang, 'Hey True Blue, don't say you've gone, say you've knocked off for a smoko and you'll be back later on … '

The truck drove away, and as zoo staff laid a bed of flowers spelling out the word Crikey, tears flowed for the Wildlife Warrior.